What are you going to Believe?

JOYCE MEYER

WHAT ARE YOU GOING TO BELIEVE?

Printed in the United States of America.

First Printing, 2013

ISBN 978-0-9754159-3-1

Joyce Meyer Ministries
P.O. Box 655
Fenton, MO 63026
joycemeyer.org

CONTENTS

What am I going to Believe about

Introduction

Throughout my years in ministry, I have often focused on teaching people the importance of renewing our mind, so we can be what God created us to be and have what He wants us to have. Romans 12:2 says, *. . . Be transformed (changed) by the [entire] renewal of your mind [by its new ideals and its new attitude], so that you may prove [for yourselves] what is the good and acceptable and perfect will of God . . . .* And Proverbs 23:7 tells us that as a man thinks in his heart, so is he. Or as I like to say, "Where the mind goes, the man follows."

Obviously, what we think and believe in our heart is vitally important in determining the quality of life we will have: Are we going to be victorious Christians, enjoying the abundant life Jesus died to give us, or will we settle for a mediocre, constantly struggling, barely-getting-by kind of life?

What we choose to believe determines our faith and affects every area of our life: salvation (Romans 10:9; Acts 16:31), answered prayer (Matthew 21:22), receiving blessings (Galatians 3:22), overcoming fear (Mark 5:36), righteousness (Genesis 15:6), and so much more.

The truth is, when you believe the wrong things about your life, your life will go in the wrong direction. But when you begin to think and believe what God says about you, you will experience new levels of victory in every area of your life.

It is important to note that our thoughts are never the source of our joy, peace or victory—God is the ultimate Source of every good thing in our lives. But as we choose to line up our beliefs with God's Word, the power of His Word changes us for the better (see Hebrews 4:12; Isaiah 55:11).

We've put this book together to help encourage you with promises from God's Word—promises that apply to every area of your life. So in each section, you'll find several "Think It, Say It" statements, based on the Word, that you can use as personal confessions for your life. The "Believe It" categories list scriptures that support those statements.

The power we need to live a victorious life in Christ is found in God's Word, so it's vitally important that what we believe is grounded in Scripture. No matter what you are facing today, you can believe what God has spoken, and you can begin to really enjoy the life He has given you.

Believing is more than just wishful thinking. It is a process that includes the thoughts you choose to dwell on, the words you choose to speak about your future, and the actions you choose to take. That's why each section of this book will equip you to think, speak and believe God's promises.

Remember: Where the mind goes, the man follows. So make the decision to believe God's promises today. I can tell you from my own life experience—it's the key to having the life you long to have!

Joyce

Seek the Lord and His strength; yearn for and seek His face and to be in His presence continually!

1 CHRONICLES 16:11

CHAPTER 1

What am I going to Believe about

GOD?

The proper understanding and belief about God is something that will greatly benefit every area of your life. When you know who He is and see how He works in Scripture, you can learn to trust Him in ways you hadn't before.

Though God is holy and is to be worshiped, He is not aloof and distant from us. He loves each one of us and desires to have a deep and intimate relationship with us.

If you have struggled at times in your understanding of who God is, allow the scriptures in this section to shape your beliefs about your heavenly Father.

THINK IT, SAY IT: ***Because God loves me, I can live in relationship with Him and seek Him with all my heart.***

BELIEVE IT:

But if from there you will seek (inquire for and require as necessity) the Lord your God, you will find Him if you [truly] seek Him with all your heart [and mind] and soul and life.

DEUTERONOMY 4:29

I love those who love me, and those who seek me early and diligently shall find me.

PROVERBS 8:17

Then you will call upon Me, and you will come and pray to Me, and I will hear and heed you. Then you will seek Me, inquire for, and require Me [as a vital necessity] and find Me when you search for Me with all your heart.

JEREMIAH 29:12-13

The Lord is good to those who wait hopefully and expectantly for Him, to those who seek Him [inquire of and for Him and require Him by right of necessity and on the authority of God's word].

LAMENTATIONS 3:25

Seek, inquire for, and require the Lord while He may be found [claiming Him by necessity and by right]; call upon Him while He is near.
ISAIAH 55:6

With my whole heart have I sought You, inquiring for and of You and yearning for You; Oh, let me not wander or step aside [either in ignorance or willfully] from Your commandments. Your word have I laid up in my heart, that I might not sin against You.
PSALM 119:10-11

Seek the Lord and His strength; yearn for and seek His face and to be in His presence continually!
1 CHRONICLES 16:11

The young lions lack food and suffer hunger, but they who seek (inquire of and require) the Lord [by right of their need and on the authority of His Word], none of them shall lack any beneficial thing.
PSALM 34:10

But seek (aim at and strive after) first of all His kingdom and His righteousness (His way of doing and being right), and then all these things taken together will be given you besides.
MATTHEW 6:33

Let all those that seek and require You rejoice and be glad in You; let such as love Your salvation say continually, The Lord be magnified!
PSALM 40:16

As for me, I would seek God and inquire of and require Him, and to God would I commit my cause—Who does great things and unsearchable, marvelous things without number.

JOB 5:8-9

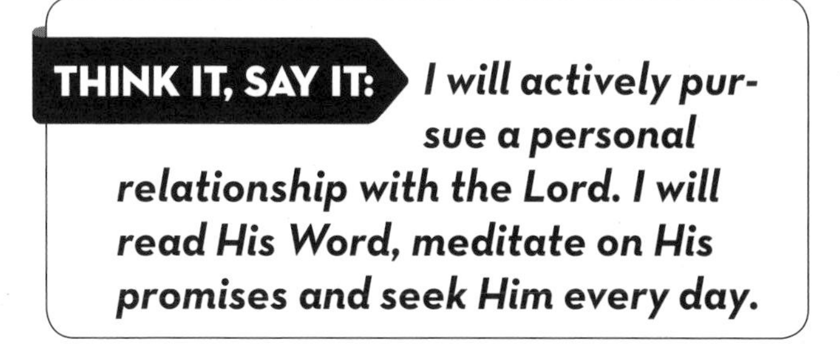

BELIEVE IT:

O God, You are my God, earnestly will I seek You; my inner self thirsts for You, my flesh longs and is faint for You, in a dry and weary land where no water is.

PSALM 63:1

And they who know Your name [who have experience and acquaintance with Your mercy] will lean on and confidently put their trust in You, for You, Lord, have not forsaken those who seek (inquire of and for) You [on the authority of God's Word and the right of their necessity].

PSALM 9:10

And He made from one [common origin, one source, one blood] all nations of men to settle on the face of the earth, having definitely determined [their] allotted periods of time and the fixed boundaries of their habitation (their settlements, lands, and abodes), so that they should seek God, in the hope that they might feel after Him and find Him, although He is not far from each one of us.

ACTS 17:26-27

But without faith it is impossible to please and be satisfactory to Him. For whoever would come near to God must [necessarily] believe that God exists and that He is the rewarder of those who earnestly and diligently seek Him [out].

HEBREWS 11:6

Blessed (happy, fortunate, to be envied) are they who keep His testimonies, and who seek, inquire for and of Him and crave Him with the whole heart.

PSALM 119:2

The Lord looked down from heaven upon the children of men to see if there were any who understood, dealt wisely, and sought after God, inquiring for and of Him and requiring Him [of vital necessity].

PSALM 14:2

And whatever you do [no matter what it is] in word or deed, do everything in the name of the Lord Jesus and in [dependence upon] His Person, giving praise to God the Father through Him.

COLOSSIANS 3:17

Come close to God and He will come close to you . . . .
JAMES 4:8

You have said, Seek My face [inquire for and require My presence as your vital need]. My heart says to You, Your face (Your presence), Lord, will I seek, inquire for, and require [of necessity and on the authority of Your Word].
PSALM 27:8

As the hart pants and longs for the water brooks, so I pant and long for You, O God. My inner self thirsts for God, for the living God. When shall I come and behold the face of God?
PSALM 42:1-2

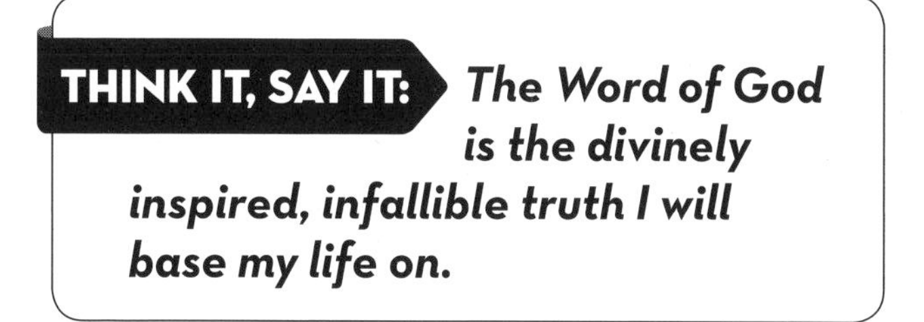

BELIEVE IT:

For no prophecy ever originated because some man willed it [to do so—it never came by human impulse], but men spoke from God who were borne along (moved and impelled) by the Holy Spirit.
2 PETER 1:21

Every Scripture is God-breathed (given by His inspiration) and profitable for instruction, for reproof and conviction of sin, for correction of error and discipline in obedience, [and] for training in righteousness (in holy living, in conformity to God's will in thought, purpose, and action), so that the man of God may be complete and proficient, well fitted and thoroughly equipped for every good work.

2 TIMOTHY 3:16-17

Sanctify them [purify, consecrate, separate them for Yourself, make them holy] by the Truth; Your Word is Truth.

JOHN 17:17

This Book of the Law shall not depart out of your mouth, but you shall meditate on it day and night, that you may observe and do according to all that is written in it. For then you shall make your way prosperous, and then you shall deal wisely and have good success.

JOSHUA 1:8

The law of the Lord is perfect, restoring the [whole] person; the testimony of the Lord is sure, making wise the simple. The precepts of the Lord are right, rejoicing the heart; the commandment of the Lord is pure and bright, enlightening the eyes. The [reverent] fear of the Lord is clean, enduring forever; the ordinances of the Lord are true and righteous altogether. More to be desired are they than gold, even than much fine gold; they are sweeter also than honey and drippings from the honeycomb. Moreover, by them is Your servant warned (reminded, illuminated, and instructed); and in keeping them there is great reward.

PSALM 19:7-11

So Jesus said to those Jews who had believed in Him, If you abide in My word [hold fast to My teachings and live in accordance with them], you are truly My disciples. And you will know the Truth, and the Truth will set you free.

JOHN 8:31-32

And He humbled you and allowed you to hunger and fed you with manna, which you did not know nor did your fathers know, that He might make you recognize and personally know that man does not live by bread only, but man lives by every word that proceeds out of the mouth of the Lord.

DEUTERONOMY 8:3

Forever, O Lord, Your word is settled in heaven [stands firm as the heavens].

PSALM 119:89

I will meditate on Your precepts and have respect to Your ways [the paths of life marked out by Your law]. I will delight myself in Your statutes; I will not forget Your word.

PSALM 119:15-16

God's promises and instructions are trustworthy and true. I can live in peace and security, knowing He has my life in His hands.

BELIEVE IT:

Lean on, trust in, and be confident in the Lord with all your heart and mind and do not rely on your own insight or understanding. In all your ways know, recognize, and acknowledge Him, and He will direct and make straight and plain your paths.

PROVERBS 3:5-6

Commit your way to the Lord [roll and repose each care of your load on Him]; trust (lean on, rely on, and be confident) also in Him and He will bring it to pass.

PSALM 37:5

The Lord is my Strength and my [impenetrable] Shield; my heart trusts in, relies on, and confidently leans on Him, and I am helped; therefore my heart greatly rejoices, and with my song will I praise Him.

PSALM 28:7

For I am the Lord, I do not change; that is why you, O sons of Jacob, are not consumed.

MALACHI 3:6

And they who know Your name [who have experience and acquaintance with Your mercy] will lean on and confidently put their trust in You, for You, Lord, have not forsaken those who seek (inquire of and for) You [on the authority of God's Word and the right of their necessity].
PSALM 9:10

But the Comforter (Counselor, Helper, Intercessor, Advocate, Strengthener, Standby), the Holy Spirit, Whom the Father will send in My name [in My place, to represent Me and act on My behalf], He will teach you all things. And He will cause you to recall (will remind you of, bring to your remembrance) everything I have told you.
JOHN 14:26

He shall not be afraid of evil tidings; his heart is firmly fixed, trusting (leaning on and being confident) in the Lord.
PSALM 112:7

Jesus Christ (the Messiah) is [always] the same, yesterday, today, [yes] and forever (to the ages).
HEBREWS 13:8

You will guard him and keep him in perfect and constant peace whose mind [both its inclination and its character] is stayed on You, because he commits himself to You, leans on You, and hopes confidently in You.
ISAIAH 26:3

Some trust in and boast of chariots and some of horses, but we will trust in and boast of the name of the Lord our God.

PSALM 20:7

I don't have to try to figure things out on my own. I will live my life, trusting God and the destiny He has for me.

BELIEVE IT:

For in Him does our heart rejoice, because we have trusted (relied on and been confident) in His holy name.

PSALM 33:21

So that we who first hoped in Christ [who first put our confidence in Him have been destined and appointed to] live for the praise of His glory!

EPHESIANS 1:12

Do not let your hearts be troubled (distressed, agitated). You believe in and adhere to and trust in and rely on God; believe in and adhere to and trust in and rely also on Me.

JOHN 14:1

Offer just and right sacrifices; trust (lean on and be confident) in the Lord.

PSALM 4:5

But I trusted in, relied on, and was confident in You, O Lord; I said, You are my God. My times are in Your hands; deliver me from the hands of my foes and those who pursue me and persecute me. Let Your face shine on Your servant; save me for Your mercy's sake and in Your loving-kindness.

PSALM 31:14-16

For I will not trust in and lean on my bow, neither shall my sword save me. But You have saved us from our foes and have put them to shame who hate us. In God we have made our boast all the day long, and we will give thanks to Your name forever. Selah [pause, and calmly think of that]!

PSALM 44:6-8

What time I am afraid, I will have confidence in and put my trust and reliance in You. By [the help of] God I will praise His word; on God I lean, rely, and confidently put my trust; I will not fear. What can man, who is flesh, do to me?

PSALM 56:3-4

For You are my hope; O Lord God, You are my trust from my youth and the source of my confidence.

PSALM 71:5

In God have I put my trust and confident reliance; I will not be afraid. What can man do to me? Your vows are upon me, O God; I will render praise to You and give You thank offerings. For You have delivered my life from death, yes, and my feet from falling, that I may walk before God in the light of life and of the living.

PSALM 56:11-13

But [God] led His own people forth like sheep and guided them [with a shepherd's care] like a flock in the wilderness. And He led them on safely and in confident trust, so that they feared not; but the sea overwhelmed their enemies.

PSALM 78:52-53

... He who puts his trust in the Lord shall be enriched and blessed.

PROVERBS 28:25

As He said these things, many believed in Him [trusted, relied on, and adhered to Him].

JOHN 8:30

For the vision is yet for an appointed time and it hastens to the end [fulfillment]; it will not deceive or disappoint. Though it tarry, wait [earnestly] for it, because it will surely come; it will not be behindhand on its appointed day.

HABAKKUK 2:3

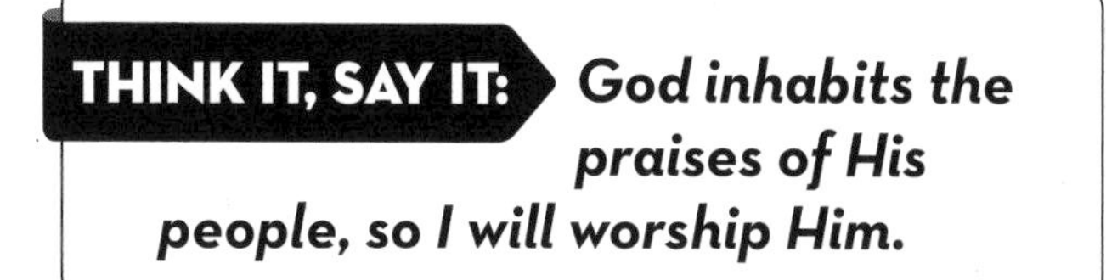

BELIEVE IT:

But You are holy, O You Who dwell in [the holy place where] the praises of Israel [are offered].
PSALM 22:3

I will extol You, my God, O King; and I will bless Your name forever and ever [with grateful, affectionate praise]. Every day [with its new reasons] will I bless You [affectionately and gratefully praise You]; yes, I will praise Your name forever and ever.
PSALM 145:1-2

Praise the Lord! Praise God in His sanctuary; praise Him in the heavens of His power! Praise Him for His mighty acts; praise Him according to the abundance of His greatness!
PSALM 150:1-2

Through Him, therefore, let us constantly and at all times offer up to God a sacrifice of praise, which is the fruit of lips that thankfully acknowledge and confess and glorify His name.
HEBREWS 13:15

Serve the Lord with gladness! Come before His presence with singing! Know (perceive, recognize, and understand with approval) that the Lord is God! It is He Who has made us, not we ourselves [and we are His]! We are His people and the sheep of His pasture.

PSALM 100:2-3

A time will come, however, indeed it is already here, when the true (genuine) worshipers will worship the Father in spirit and in truth (reality); for the Father is seeking just such people as these as His worshipers.

JOHN 4:23

Let be and be still, and know (recognize and understand) that I am God. I will be exalted among the nations! I will be exalted in the earth!

PSALM 46:10

Enter into His gates with thanksgiving and a thank offering and into His courts with praise! Be thankful and say so to Him, bless and affectionately praise His name!

PSALM 100:4

O come, let us sing to the Lord; let us make a joyful noise to the Rock of our salvation! Let us come before His presence with thanksgiving; let us make a joyful noise to Him with songs of praise! For the Lord is a great God, and a great King above all gods.

PSALM 95:1-3

Let everything that has breath and every breath of life praise the Lord! Praise the Lord! (Hallelujah!)

PSALM 150:6

Lord, I love You, and I worship You for who You are and what You have done in my life.

BELIEVE IT:

Speak out to one another in psalms and hymns and spiritual songs, offering praise with voices [and instruments] and making melody with all your heart to the Lord.

EPHESIANS 5:19

And call on Me in the day of trouble; I will deliver you, and you shall honor and glorify Me.

PSALM 50:15

Praise the Lord! (Hallelujah!) Praise the Lord, O my soul! While I live will I praise the Lord; I will sing praises to my God while I have any being.

PSALM 146:1-2

O praise the Lord, all you nations! Praise Him, all you people!

PSALM 117:1

Let the heavens be glad and let the earth rejoice; and let men say among the nations, The Lord reigns! Let the sea roar, and all the things that fill it; let the fields rejoice, and all that is in them. Then shall the trees of the wood sing out for joy before the Lord, for He comes to judge and govern the earth.
1 CHRONICLES 16:31-33

O sing to the Lord a new song; sing to the Lord, all the earth! Sing to the Lord, bless (affectionately praise) His name; show forth His salvation from day to day.
PSALM 96:1-2

I will give to the Lord the thanks due to His rightness and justice, and I will sing praise to the name of the Lord Most High.
PSALM 7:17

Great is the Lord and highly to be praised; and His greatness is [so vast and deep as to be] unsearchable. One generation shall laud Your works to another and shall declare Your mighty acts. On the glorious splendor of Your majesty and on Your wondrous works I will meditate.
PSALM 145:3-5

And David and all Israel merrily celebrated before God with all their might, with songs and lyres and harps and tambourines and cymbals and trumpets.
1 CHRONICLES 13:8

BELIEVE IT:

But about midnight, as Paul and Silas were praying and singing hymns of praise to God, and the [other] prisoners were listening to them, suddenly there was a great earthquake, so that the very foundations of the prison were shaken; and at once all the doors were opened and everyone's shackles were unfastened.

ACTS 16:25-26

Declare His glory among the nations, His marvelous works among all the peoples. For great is the Lord and greatly to be praised; He is to be reverently feared and worshiped above all [so-called] gods.

PSALM 96:3-4

Ascribe to the Lord the glory due His name. Bring an offering and come before Him; worship the Lord in the beauty of holiness and in holy array.

1 CHRONICLES 16:29

I call on the Lord, Who is worthy to be praised, and I am saved from my enemies.

2 SAMUEL 22:4

Yet Jesus has been considered worthy of much greater honor and glory than Moses, just as the builder of a house has more honor than the house [itself].
HEBREWS 3:3

To the one only God, our Savior through Jesus Christ our Lord, be glory (splendor), majesty, might and dominion, and power and authority, before all time and now and forever (unto all the ages of eternity). Amen (so be it).
JUDE 1:25

Make a joyful noise unto God, all the earth; Sing forth the honor and glory of His name; make His praise glorious! Say to God, How awesome and fearfully glorious are Your works! Through the greatness of Your power shall Your enemies submit themselves to You [with feigned and reluctant obedience]. All the earth shall bow down to You and sing [praises] to You; they shall praise Your name in song . . . .
PSALM 66:1-4

Extol the Lord our God and worship at His footstool! Holy is He!
PSALM 99:5

[And Ezra said], You are the Lord, You alone; You have made heaven, the heaven of heavens, with all their host, the earth, and all that is on it, the seas and all that is in them; and You preserve them all, and the hosts of heaven worship You.
NEHEMIAH 9:6

THINK IT, SAY IT: ***The power of God can deliver me from any situation I might face.***

BELIEVE IT:

God has spoken once, twice have I heard this: that power belongs to God.

PSALM 62:11

Little children, you are of God [you belong to Him] and have [already] defeated and overcome them [the agents of the antichrist], because He Who lives in you is greater (mightier) than he who is in the world.

1 JOHN 4:4

And God both raised the Lord to life and will also raise us up by His power.

1 CORINTHIANS 6:14

With a strong hand and with an outstretched arm, for His mercy and loving-kindness endure forever.

PSALM 136:12

So trust in the Lord (commit yourself to Him, lean on Him, hope confidently in Him) forever; for the Lord God is an everlasting Rock [the Rock of Ages].

ISAIAH 26:4

Yet these are but [a small part of His doings] the outskirts of His ways or the mere fringes of His force, the faintest whisper of His voice! Who dares contemplate or who can understand the thunders of His full, magnificent power?

JOB 26:14

In conclusion, be strong in the Lord [be empowered through your union with Him]; draw your strength from Him [that strength which His boundless might provides].

EPHESIANS 6:10

The Lord is my rescuer. I have nothing to fear.

BELIEVE IT:

God is our Refuge and Strength [mighty and impenetrable to temptation], a very present and well-proved help in trouble.

PSALM 46:1

[Then] He will cover you with His pinions, and under His wings shall you trust and find refuge; His truth and His faithfulness are a shield and a buckler.

PSALM 91:4

I will call upon the Lord, Who is to be praised; so shall I be saved from my enemies.
PSALM 18:3

When you pass through the waters, I will be with you, and through the rivers, they will not overwhelm you. When you walk through the fire, you will not be burned or scorched, nor will the flame kindle upon you. For I am the Lord your God, the Holy One of Israel, your Savior . . . .
ISAIAH 43:2-3

This poor man cried, and the Lord heard him, and saved him out of all his troubles.
PSALM 34:6

There is no fear in love [dread does not exist], but full-grown (complete, perfect) love turns fear out of doors and expels every trace of terror! For fear brings with it the thought of punishment, and [so] he who is afraid has not reached the full maturity of love [is not yet grown into love's complete perfection].
1 JOHN 4:18

[For it is He] Who rescued and saved us from such a perilous death, and He will still rescue and save us; in and on Him we have set our hope (our joyful and confident expectation) that He will again deliver us [from danger and destruction and draw us to Himself]
2 CORINTHIANS 1:10

When worry, fear or anxiety try to take root in my life, I will remember that God is on my side, and He will provide everything I need.

BELIEVE IT:

The Lord is their [unyielding] Strength, and He is the Stronghold of salvation to [me] His anointed. Save Your people and bless Your heritage; nourish and shepherd them and carry them forever.

PSALM 28:8-9

I have been young and now am old, yet have I not seen the [uncompromisingly] righteous forsaken or their seed begging bread.

PSALM 37:25

And said, I cried out of my distress to the Lord, and He heard me; out of the belly of Sheol cried I, and You heard my voice.

JONAH 2:2

In my distress I called upon the Lord; I cried to my God, and He heard my voice from His temple; my cry came into His ears.

2 SAMUEL 22:7

My eyes are ever toward the Lord, for He will pluck my feet out of the net.

PSALM 25:15

He drew me up out of a horrible pit [a pit of tumult and of destruction], out of the miry clay (froth and slime), and set my feet upon a rock, steadying my steps and establishing my goings.

PSALM 40:2

I will say of the Lord, He is my Refuge and my Fortress, my God; on Him I lean and rely, and in Him I [confidently] trust!

PSALM 91:2

. . . Behold, I am with you all the days (perpetually, uniformly, and on every occasion), to the [very] close and consummation of the age. Amen (so let it be).

MATTHEW 28:20

The Lord is near to all who call upon Him, to all who call upon Him sincerely and in truth.

PSALM 145:18

Put on God's whole armor [the armor of a heavy-armed soldier which God supplies], that you may be able successfully to stand up against [all] the strategies and the deceits of the devil.

EPHESIANS 6:11

God is majestic in His sovereignty. He has no equal and is worthy of my reverence and honor.

BELIEVE IT:

And His mercy (His compassion and kindness toward the miserable and afflicted) is on those who fear Him with godly reverence, from generation to generation and age to age.

LUKE 1:50

The reverent fear and worshipful awe of the Lord [includes] the hatred of evil; pride, arrogance, the evil way, and perverted and twisted speech I hate.

PROVERBS 8:13

The reverent and worshipful fear of the Lord is the beginning and the principal and choice part of knowledge [its starting point and its essence]; but fools despise skillful and godly Wisdom, instruction, and discipline.

PROVERBS 1:7

All has been heard; the end of the matter is: Fear God [revere and worship Him, knowing that He is] and keep His commandments, for this is the whole

of man [the full, original purpose of his creation, the object of God's providence, the root of character, the foundation of all happiness, the adjustment to all inharmonious circumstances and conditions under the sun] and the whole [duty] for every man.
ECCLESIASTES 12:13

Let all the earth fear the Lord [revere and worship Him]; let all the inhabitants of the world stand in awe of Him.
PSALM 33:8

In the reverent and worshipful fear of the Lord there is strong confidence, and His children shall always have a place of refuge.
PROVERBS 14:26

The secret [of the sweet, satisfying companionship] of the Lord have they who fear (revere and worship) Him, and He will show them His covenant and reveal to them its [deep, inner] meaning.
PSALM 25:14

But to man He said, Behold, the reverential and worshipful fear of the Lord—that is Wisdom; and to depart from evil is understanding.
JOB 28:28

Reverent and worshipful fear of the Lord is a fountain of life, that one may avoid the snares of death.
PROVERBS 14:27

Be not wise in your own eyes; reverently fear and worship the Lord and turn [entirely] away from evil.
PROVERBS 3:7

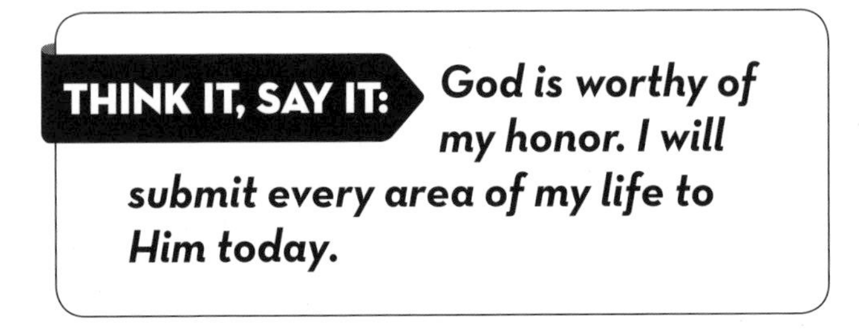

BELIEVE IT:

Teach me Your way, O Lord, that I may walk and live in Your truth; direct and unite my heart [solely, reverently] to fear and honor Your name.
PSALM 86:11

And now, Israel, what does the Lord your God require of you but [reverently] to fear the Lord your God, [that is] to walk in all His ways, and to love Him, and to serve the Lord your God with all your [mind and] heart and with your entire being.
DEUTERONOMY 10:12

I appeal to you therefore, brethren, and beg of you in view of [all] the mercies of God, to make a decisive dedication of your bodies [presenting all your members and faculties] as a living sacrifice, holy (devoted, consecrated) and well pleasing to

God, which is your reasonable (rational, intelligent) service and spiritual worship.
ROMANS 12:1

By mercy and love, truth and fidelity [to God and man—not by sacrificial offerings], iniquity is purged out of the heart, and by the reverent, worshipful fear of the Lord men depart from and avoid evil.
PROVERBS 16:6

Show respect for all men [treat them honorably]. Love the brotherhood (the Christian fraternity of which Christ is the Head). Reverence God . . . .
1 PETER 2:17

Behold, the heavens and the heaven of heavens belong to the Lord your God, the earth also, with all that is in it and on it.
DEUTERONOMY 10:14

But in every nation he who venerates and has a reverential fear for God, treating Him with worshipful obedience and living uprightly, is acceptable to Him and sure of being received and welcomed [by Him].
ACTS 10:35

Praise the Lord! (Hallelujah!) Blessed (happy, fortunate, to be envied) is the man who fears (reveres and worships) the Lord, who delights greatly in His commandments.
PSALM 112:1

The reverent fear and worship of the Lord is the beginning of Wisdom and skill [the preceding and the first essential, the prerequisite and the alphabet]; a good understanding, wisdom, and meaning have all those who do [the will of the Lord]. Their praise of Him endures forever.

PSALM 111:10

Oh, that they had such a [mind and] heart in them always [reverently] to fear Me and keep all My commandments, that it might go well with them and with their children forever!

DEUTERONOMY 5:29

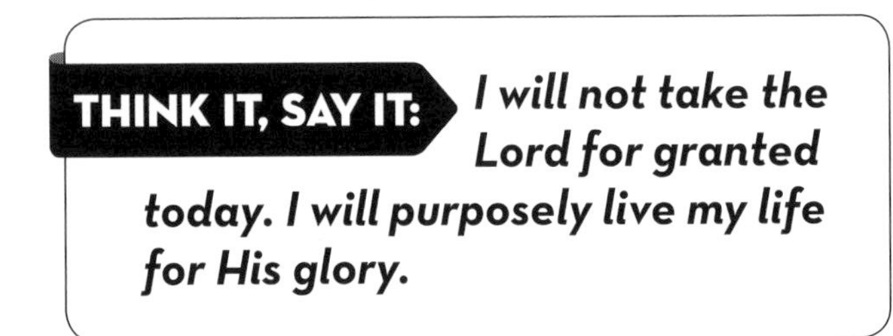

BELIEVE IT:

So the church throughout the whole of Judea and Galilee and Samaria had peace and was edified [growing in wisdom, virtue, and piety] and walking in the respect and reverential fear of the Lord and in the consolation and exhortation of the Holy Spirit, continued to increase and was multiplied.

ACTS 9:31

If you [really] love Me, you will keep (obey) My commands.
JOHN 14:15

I know that whatever God does, it endures forever; nothing can be added to it nor anything taken from it. And God does it so that men will [reverently] fear Him [revere and worship Him, knowing that He is].
ECCLESIASTES 3:14

Charm and grace are deceptive, and beauty is vain [because it is not lasting], but a woman who reverently and worshipfully fears the Lord, she shall be praised!
PROVERBS 31:30

O fear the Lord, you His saints [revere and worship Him]! For there is no want to those who truly revere and worship Him with godly fear.
PSALM 34:9

Now therefore, [reverently] fear the Lord and serve Him in sincerity and in truth; put away the gods which your fathers served . . . and serve the Lord.
JOSHUA 24:14

Be subject to one another out of reverence for Christ (the Messiah, the Anointed One).
EPHESIANS 5:21

And shall make Him of quick understanding, and His delight shall be in the reverential and obedient fear of the Lord. And He shall not judge by the sight of His eyes, neither decide by the hearing of His ears.

ISAIAH 11:3

Blessed (happy, fortunate, to be envied) is everyone who fears, reveres, and worships the Lord, who walks in His ways and lives according to His commandments.

PSALM 128:1

The reward of humility and the reverent and worshipful fear of the Lord is riches and honor and life.

PROVERBS 22:4

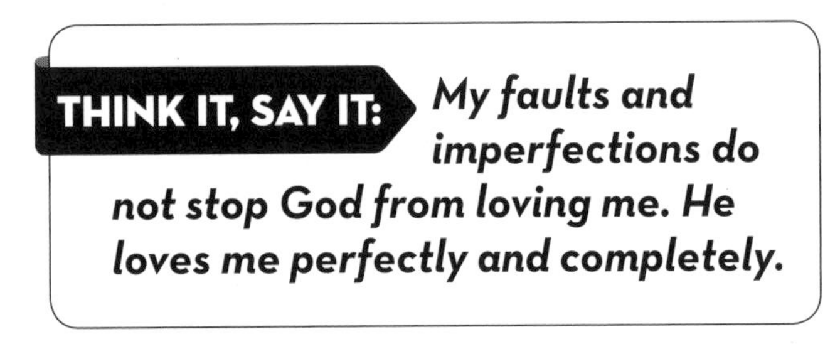

BELIEVE IT:

May Christ through your faith [actually] dwell (settle down, abide, make His permanent home) in your hearts! May you be rooted deep in love and founded securely on love, that you may have the power and be strong to apprehend and grasp with all the saints [God's devoted people, the experience of that love] what is the breadth and length and height and depth [of it].

EPHESIANS 3:17-18

And we know (understand, recognize, are conscious of, by observation and by experience) and believe (adhere to and put faith in and rely on) the love God cherishes for us. God is love, and he who dwells and continues in love dwells and continues in God, and God dwells and continues in him.
1 JOHN 4:16

We love Him, because He first loved us.
1 JOHN 4:19

For I am persuaded beyond doubt (am sure) that neither death nor life, nor angels nor principalities, nor things impending and threatening nor things to come, nor powers, nor height nor depth, nor anything else in all creation will be able to separate us from the love of God which is in Christ Jesus our Lord.
ROMANS 8:38-39

[That you may really come] to know [practically, through experience for yourselves] the love of Christ, which far surpasses mere knowledge [without experience]; that you may be filled [through all your being] unto all the fullness of God [may have the richest measure of the divine Presence, and become a body wholly filled and flooded with God Himself]!
EPHESIANS 3:19

The Lord is merciful and gracious, slow to anger and plenteous in mercy and loving-kindness.
PSALM 103:8

The Lord appeared from of old to me [Israel], saying, Yes, I have loved you with an everlasting love; therefore with loving-kindness have I drawn you and continued My faithfulness to you.

JEREMIAH 31:3

As a father loves and pities his children, so the Lord loves and pities those who fear Him [with reverence, worship, and awe].

PSALM 103:13

Behold, I have indelibly imprinted (tattooed a picture of) you on the palm of each of My hands; [O Zion] your walls are continually before Me.

ISAIAH 49:16

For in Christ Jesus you are all sons of God through faith.

GALATIANS 3:26

CHAPTER 2

What am I going to Believe about MYSELF?

Knowing who you are in Christ is one of the most important, foundational truths in the life of a believer. This is why God reminds us repeatedly in His Word that we are found in Him and have hope for a great future.

Too many times we believe the lies of the enemy about our identity. This misconception of who we are causes us to live with less than God's best for our lives.

If we really saw ourselves as God sees us—loved, accepted, overcoming, victorious, righteous, forgiven, blessed—we would live our lives with a newfound sense of confidence and purpose.

You don't have to believe the lies you've been told about yourself any longer. You can stand on the truth of God's Word and choose to believe what He says about you is true. No matter what you've done or what you've been through, you are a new creation in Christ. Your purpose, self-worth and identity are all beautiful and complete because they are all found in Christ.

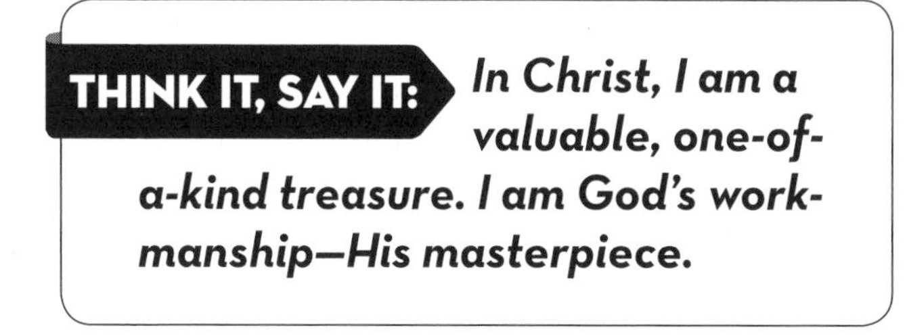

BELIEVE IT:

For we are God's [own] handiwork (His workmanship), recreated in Christ Jesus, [born anew] that we may do those good works which God predestined (planned beforehand) for us [taking paths which He prepared ahead of time], that we should walk in them [living the good life which He prearranged and made ready for us to live].

EPHESIANS 2:10

For You formed my inward parts; You covered me in my mother's womb. I will praise You, for I am fearfully and wonderfully made; marvelous are Your works, And that my soul knows very well.

PSALMS 139:13-14 NKJV

He has made everything beautiful in its time. He also has planted eternity in men's hearts and minds [a divinely implanted sense of a purpose working through the ages which nothing under the sun but God alone can satisfy] . . . .

ECCLESIASTES 3:11

Thus says the Lord, Who made you and formed you from the womb, Who will help you: Fear not, O Jacob, My servant, and you Jeshurun [the upright one—applied to Israel as a type of the Messiah], whom I have chosen.

ISAIAH 44:2

Do you not know that your body is the temple (the very sanctuary) of the Holy Spirit Who lives within you, Whom you have received [as a Gift] from God? . . .

1 CORINTHIANS 6:19

May blessing (praise, laudation, and eulogy) be to the God and Father of our Lord Jesus Christ (the Messiah) Who has blessed us in Christ with every spiritual (given by the Holy Spirit) blessing in the heavenly realm!

EPHESIANS 1:3

But we are citizens of the state (commonwealth, homeland) which is in heaven, and from it also we earnestly and patiently await [the coming of] the Lord Jesus Christ (the Messiah) [as] Savior.

PHILIPPIANS 3:20

THINK IT, SAY IT: ***I have been uniquely created in the image of God.***

BELIEVE IT:

So God created man in His own image, in the image and likeness of God He created him; male and female He created them.

GENESIS 1:27

And God saw everything that He had made, and behold, it was very good (suitable, pleasant) and He approved it completely . . . .

GENESIS 1:31

. . . Thus says the Lord, He Who created you, O Jacob, and He Who formed you, O Israel: Fear not, for I have redeemed you [ransomed you by paying a price instead of leaving you captives]; I have called you by your name; you are Mine.

ISAIAH 43:1

For it was in Him that all things were created, in heaven and on earth, things seen and things unseen, whether thrones, dominions, rulers, or authorities; all things were created and exist through Him [by His service, intervention] and in and for Him.

COLOSSIANS 1:16

I will choose to see myself as a child of God. In every situation I face, I will live in the love and protection of my heavenly Father.

BELIEVE IT:

The Spirit Himself [thus] testifies together with our own spirit, [assuring us] that we are children of God.

ROMANS 8:16

See what [an incredible] quality of love the Father has given (shown, bestowed on) us, that we should [be permitted to] be named and called and counted the children of God! And so we are! The reason that the world does not know (recognize, acknowledge) us is that it does not know (recognize, acknowledge) Him.

1 JOHN 3:1

But to as many as did receive and welcome Him, He gave the authority (power, privilege, right) to become the children of God, that is, to those who believe in (adhere to, trust in, and rely on) His name.

JOHN 1:12

For in Christ Jesus you are all sons of God through faith.

GALATIANS 3:26

For [the Spirit which] you have now received [is] not a spirit of slavery to put you once more in bondage to fear, but you have received the Spirit of adoption [the Spirit producing sonship] in [the bliss of] which we cry, Abba (Father)! Father!

ROMANS 8:15

And if we are [His] children, then we are [His] heirs also: heirs of God and fellow heirs with Christ [sharing His inheritance with Him]; only we must share His suffering if we are to share His glory.

ROMANS 8:17

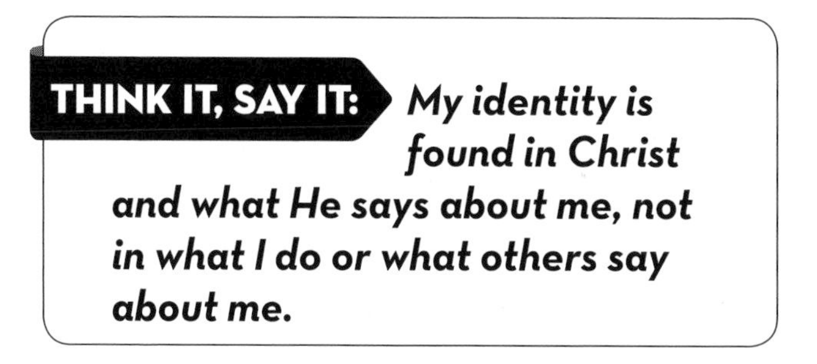

BELIEVE IT:

Therefore if any person is [ingrafted] in Christ (the Messiah) he is a new creation (a new creature altogether); the old [previous moral and spiritual condition] has passed away. Behold, the fresh and new has come!

2 CORINTHIANS 5:17

Now you [collectively] are Christ's body and [individually] you are members of it, each part severally and distinct [each with his own place and function].

1 CORINTHIANS 12:27

But you are a chosen generation, a royal priesthood, a holy nation, His own special people, that you may proclaim the praises of Him who called you out of darkness into His marvelous light.

1 PETER 2:9 NKJV

Once you were not a people [at all], but now you are God's people; once you were unpitied, but now you are pitied and have received mercy.

1 PETER 2:10

And you are in Him, made full and having come to fullness of life [in Christ you too are filled with the Godhead—Father, Son and Holy Spirit—and reach full spiritual stature]. And He is the Head of all rule and authority [of every angelic principality and power].

COLOSSIANS 2:10

Now am I trying to win the favor of men, or of God? Do I seek to please men? If I were still seeking popularity with men, I should not be a bond servant of Christ (the Messiah).

GALATIANS 1:10

I am a friend of God.

BELIEVE IT:

I do not call you servants (slaves) any longer, for the servant does not know what his master is doing (working out). But I have called you My friends, because I have made known to you everything that I have heard from My Father. [I have revealed to you everything that I have learned from Him.]

JOHN 15:15

A friend loves at all times . . . .

PROVERBS 17:17

No one has greater love [no one has shown stronger affection] than to lay down (give up) his own life for his friends. You are My friends if you keep on doing the things which I command you to do.

JOHN 15:13-14

. . . "Abraham believed God, and it was credited to him as righteousness," and he was called God's friend.

JOHN 15:14

As a child of God, I have the mind of Christ. I won't be overwhelmed or intimidated by any decision I may face. I will ask for His wisdom and guidance.

BELIEVE IT:

For God did not give us a spirit of timidity (of cowardice, of craven and cringing and fawning fear), but [He has given us a spirit] of power and of love and of calm and well-balanced mind and discipline and self-control.

2 TIMOTHY 1:7

For who has known or understood the mind (the counsels and purposes) of the Lord so as to guide and instruct Him and give Him knowledge? But we have the mind of Christ (the Messiah) and do hold the thoughts (feelings and purposes) of His heart.

1 CORINTHIANS 2:16

So brace up your minds; be sober (circumspect, morally alert); set your hope wholly and unchangeably on the grace (divine favor) that is coming to you when Jesus Christ (the Messiah) is revealed.

1 PETER 1:13

Let this same attitude and purpose and [humble] mind be in you which was in Christ Jesus: [Let Him be your example in humility:]

PHILIPPIANS 2:5

Do not be conformed to this world (this age), [fashioned after and adapted to its external, superficial customs], but be transformed (changed) by the [entire] renewal of your mind [by its new ideals and its new attitude], so that you may prove [for yourselves] what is the good and acceptable and perfect will of God, even the thing which is good and acceptable and perfect [in His sight for you].

ROMANS 12:2

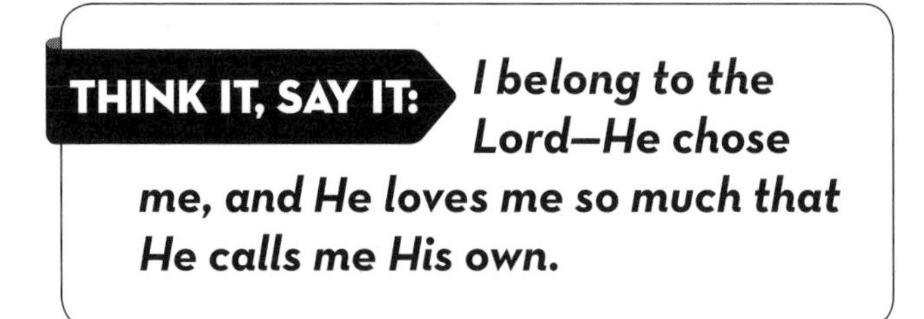

I belong to the Lord—He chose me, and He loves me so much that He calls me His own.

BELIEVE IT:

You were bought with a price [purchased with a preciousness and paid for, made His own]. So then, honor God and bring glory to Him in your body.

1 CORINTHIANS 6:20

For as many [of you] as were baptized into Christ [into a spiritual union and communion with Christ, the Anointed One, the Messiah] have put on (clothed yourselves with) Christ.
GALATIANS 3:27

Clothe yourselves therefore, as God's own chosen ones (His own picked representatives), [who are] purified and holy and well-beloved [by God Himself, by putting on behavior marked by] tenderhearted pity and mercy, kind feeling, a lowly opinion of yourselves, gentle ways, [and] patience [which is tireless and long-suffering, and has the power to endure whatever comes, with good temper].
COLOSSIANS 3:12

The earth is the Lord's, and the fullness of it, the world and they who dwell in it.
PSALM 24:1

And you are Christ's, and Christ is God's.
1 CORINTHIANS 3:23

You have not chosen Me, but I have chosen you and I have appointed you [I have planted you], that you might go and bear fruit and keep on bearing, and that your fruit may be lasting [that it may remain, abide], so that whatever you ask the Father in My Name [as presenting all that I Am], He may give it to you.
JOHN 15:16

THINK IT, SAY IT: ***Because I know who I am in Christ, I have a peace that passes understanding.***

BELIEVE IT:

And God's peace [shall be yours, that tranquil state of a soul assured of its salvation through Christ, and so fearing nothing from God and being content with its earthly lot of whatever sort that is, that peace] which transcends all understanding shall garrison and mount guard over your hearts and minds in Christ Jesus.

PHILIPPIANS 4:7

I have told you these things, so that in Me you may have [perfect] peace and confidence. In the world you have tribulation and trials and distress and frustration; but be of good cheer [take courage; be confident, certain, undaunted]! For I have overcome the world. [I have deprived it of power to harm you and have conquered it for you.]

JOHN 16:33

Peace I leave with you; My [own] peace I now give and bequeath to you. Not as the world gives do I give to you. Do not let your hearts be troubled, neither let them be afraid. [Stop allowing yourselves to be agitated and disturbed; and do not permit yourselves to be fearful and intimidated and cowardly and unsettled.]

JOHN 14:27

You will guard him and keep him in perfect and constant peace whose mind [both its inclination and its character] is stayed on You, because he commits himself to You, leans on You, and hopes confidently in You.

ISAIAH 26:3

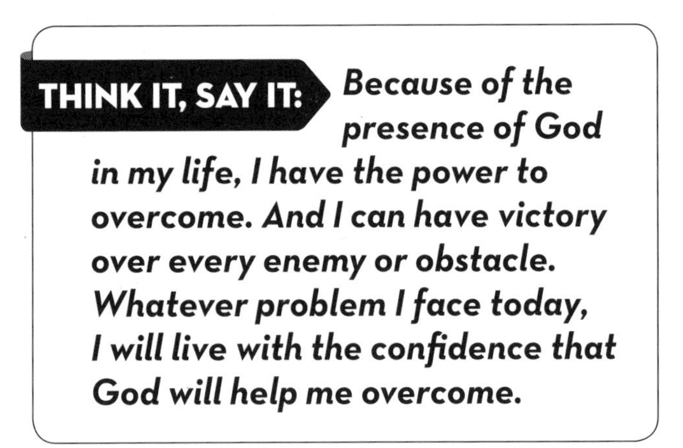

THINK IT, SAY IT: ***Because of the presence of God in my life, I have the power to overcome. And I can have victory over every enemy or obstacle. Whatever problem I face today, I will live with the confidence that God will help me overcome.***

BELIEVE IT:

I have strength for all things in Christ Who empowers me [I am ready for anything and equal to anything through Him Who infuses inner strength into me; I am self-sufficient in Christ's sufficiency].

PHILIPPIANS 4:13

Yet amid all these things we are more than conquerors and gain a surpassing victory through Him Who loved us.

ROMANS 8:37

For whatever is born of God is victorious over the world; and this is the victory that conquers the world, even our faith. Who is it that is victorious over [that conquers] the world but he who believes that Jesus is the Son of God [who adheres to, trusts in, and relies on that fact]?

1 JOHN 5:4-5

And the Lord shall make you the head, and not the tail; and you shall be above only, and you shall not be beneath, if you heed the commandments of the Lord your God which I command you this day and are watchful to do them.

DEUTERONOMY 28:13

And they overcame him by the blood of the Lamb and by the word of their testimony . . . .

REVELATION 12:11 NKJV

Do not let yourself be overcome by evil, but overcome (master) evil with good.

ROMANS 12:21

Though a host encamp against me, my heart shall not fear; though war arise against me, [even then] in this will I be confident.

PSALM 27:3

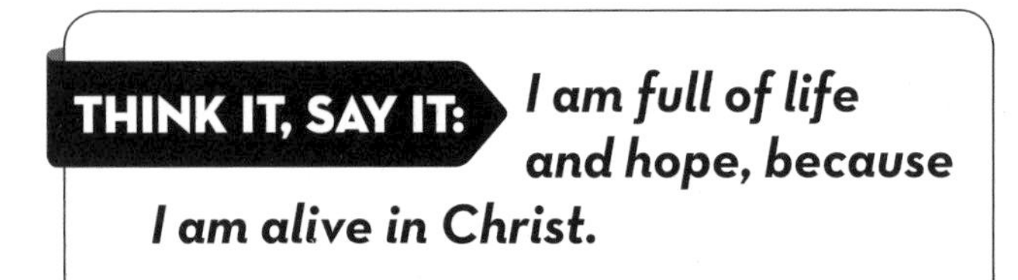

BELIEVE IT:

Even when we were dead (slain) by [our own] shortcomings and trespasses, He made us alive together in fellowship and in union with Christ; [He gave us the very life of Christ Himself, the same new life with which He quickened Him . . . .

EPHESIANS 2:5

And you [He made alive], when you were dead (slain) by [your] trespasses and sins.

EPHESIANS 2:1

Even so consider yourselves also dead to sin and your relation to it broken, but alive to God [living in unbroken fellowship with Him] in Christ Jesus.

ROMANS 6:11

Praised (honored, blessed) be the God and Father of our Lord Jesus Christ (the Messiah)! By His boundless mercy we have been born again to an ever-living hope through the resurrection of Jesus Christ from the dead.

1 PETER 1:3

If then you have been raised with Christ [to a new life, thus sharing His resurrection from the dead], aim at and seek the [rich, eternal treasures] that are above, where Christ is, seated at the right hand of God.
COLOSSIANS 3:1

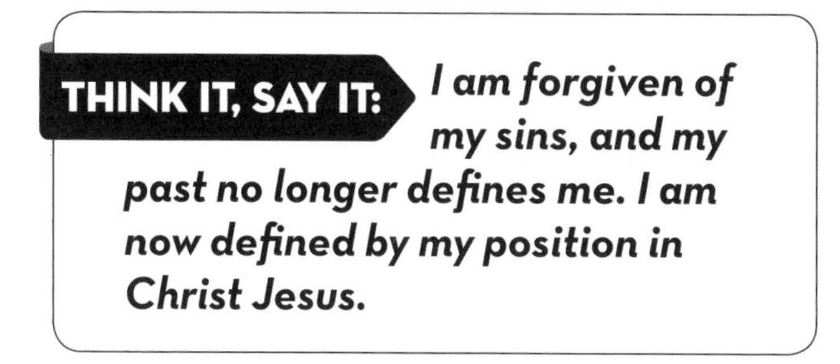

BELIEVE IT:

For God so greatly loved and dearly prized the world that He [even] gave up His only begotten (unique) Son, so that whoever believes in (trusts in, clings to, relies on) Him shall not perish (come to destruction, be lost) but have eternal (everlasting) life.
JOHN 3:16

If we [freely] admit that we have sinned and confess our sins, He is faithful and just (true to His own nature and promises) and will forgive our sins [dismiss our lawlessness] and [continuously] cleanse us from all unrighteousness [everything not in conformity to His will in purpose, thought, and action].
1 JOHN 1:9

Come now, and let us reason together, says the Lord. Though your sins are like scarlet, they shall be as white as snow; though they are red like crimson, they shall be like wool.

ISAIAH 1:18

But if we [really] are living and walking in the Light, as He [Himself] is in the Light, we have [true, unbroken] fellowship with one another, and the blood of Jesus Christ His Son cleanses (removes) us from all sin and guilt [keeps us cleansed from sin in all its forms and manifestations].

1 JOHN 1:7

For this is My blood of the new covenant, which [ratifies the agreement and] is being poured out for many for the forgiveness of sins.

MATTHEW 26:28

As far as the east is from the west, so far has He removed our transgressions from us.

PSALM 103:12

For I will be merciful and gracious toward their sins and I will remember their deeds of unrighteousness no more.

HEBREWS 8:12

He will again have compassion on us; He will subdue and tread underfoot our iniquities. You will cast all our sins into the depths of the sea.

MICAH 7:19

THINK IT, SAY IT: ***As a child of God, I will live my life with strength and confidence in Him.***

BELIEVE IT:

Be strong, courageous, and firm; fear not nor be in terror before them, for it is the Lord your God Who goes with you; He will not fail you or forsake you.
DEUTERONOMY 31:6

For the Lord your God is He Who goes with you to fight for you against your enemies to save you.
DEUTERONOMY 20:4

Also [Jesus] told them a parable to the effect that they ought always to pray and not to turn coward (faint, lose heart, and give up).
LUKE 18:1

Fear not [there is nothing to fear], for I am with you; do not look around you in terror and be dismayed, for I am your God. I will strengthen and harden you to difficulties, yes, I will help you; yes, I will hold you up and retain you with My [victorious] right hand of rightness and justice.
ISAIAH 41:10

But He said to me, My grace (My favor and loving-kindness and mercy) is enough for you [sufficient against any danger and enables you to bear the trouble manfully]; for My strength and power are made perfect (fulfilled and completed) and show themselves most effective in [your] weakness. Therefore, I will all the more gladly glory in my weaknesses and infirmities, that the strength and power of Christ (the Messiah) may rest (yes, may pitch a tent over and dwell) upon me!

2 CORINTHIANS 12:9

But those who wait for the Lord [who expect, look for, and hope in Him] shall change and renew their strength and power; they shall lift their wings and mount up [close to God] as eagles [mount up to the sun]; they shall run and not be weary, they shall walk and not faint or become tired.

ISAIAH 40:31

. . . And be not grieved and depressed, for the joy of the Lord is your strength and stronghold.

NEHEMIAH 8:10

Be strong and let your heart take courage, all you who wait for and hope for and expect the Lord!

PSALM 31:24

The Lord is my Strength and my Song, and He has become my Salvation . . . .

EXODUS 15:2

THINK IT, SAY IT: ***I am full of joy and will not give in to worry or anxiety. I will enjoy the life Jesus has given me.***

BELIEVE IT:

Rejoice and exult in hope; be steadfast and patient in suffering and tribulation; be constant in prayer.
ROMANS 12:12

May the God of your hope so fill you with all joy and peace in believing [through the experience of your faith] that by the power of the Holy Spirit you may abound and be overflowing (bubbling over) with hope.
ROMANS 15:13

Rejoice in the Lord always [delight, gladden yourselves in Him]; again I say, Rejoice!
PHILIPPIANS 4:4

[After all] the kingdom of God is not a matter of [getting the] food and drink [one likes], but instead it is righteousness (that state which makes a person acceptable to God) and [heart] peace and joy in the Holy Spirit.
ROMANS 14:17

But the fruit of the [Holy] Spirit [the work which His presence within accomplishes] is love, joy (gladness), peace, patience (an even temper, forbearance), kindness, goodness (benevolence), faithfulness, gentleness (meekness, humility), self-control (self-restraint, continence). Against such things there is no law [that can bring a charge].

GALATIANS 5:22-23

. . . Your words were to me a joy and the rejoicing of my heart, for I am called by Your name, O Lord God of hosts.

JEREMIAH 15:16

Without having seen Him, you love Him; though you do not [even] now see Him, you believe in Him and exult and thrill with inexpressible and glorious (triumphant, heavenly) joy.

1 PETER 1:8

Light is sown for the [uncompromisingly] righteous and strewn along their pathway, and joy for the upright in heart [the irrepressible joy which comes from consciousness of His favor and protection].

PSALM 97:11

The Lord will perfect that which concerns me; Your mercy and loving-kindness, O Lord, endure forever–forsake not the works of Your own hands.

PSALM 138:8

I am an ambassador for Christ, called to shine the light of God's goodness in a dark world.

BELIEVE IT:

Once more Jesus addressed the crowd. He said, I am the Light of the world. He who follows Me will not be walking in the dark, but will have the Light which is Life.

JOHN 8:12

And the Light shines on in the darkness, for the darkness has never overpowered it [put it out or absorbed it or appropriated it, and is unreceptive to it].

JOHN 1:5

So we are Christ's ambassadors, God making His appeal as it were through us. We [as Christ's personal representatives] beg you for His sake to lay hold of the divine favor [now offered you] and be reconciled to God.

2 CORINTHIANS 5:20

You are the light of the world. A city set on a hill cannot be hidden.

MATTHEW 5:14

Let your light so shine before men that they may see your moral excellence and your praiseworthy, noble, and good deeds and recognize and honor and praise and glorify your Father Who is in heaven.
MATTHEW 5:16

For once you were darkness, but now you are light in the Lord; walk as children of Light [lead the lives of those native-born to the Light].
EPHESIANS 5:8

And this is the message [the message of promise] which we have heard from Him and now are reporting to you: God is Light, and there is no darkness in Him at all [no, not in any way].
1 JOHN 1:5

The people who sat (dwelt enveloped) in darkness have seen a great Light, and for those who sat in the land and shadow of death Light has dawned.
MATTHEW 4:16

Go then and make disciples of all the nations, baptizing them into the name of the Father and of the Son and of the Holy Spirit.
MATTHEW 28:19

And He said to them, Go into all the world and preach and publish openly the good news (the Gospel) to every creature [of the whole human race].
MARK 16:15

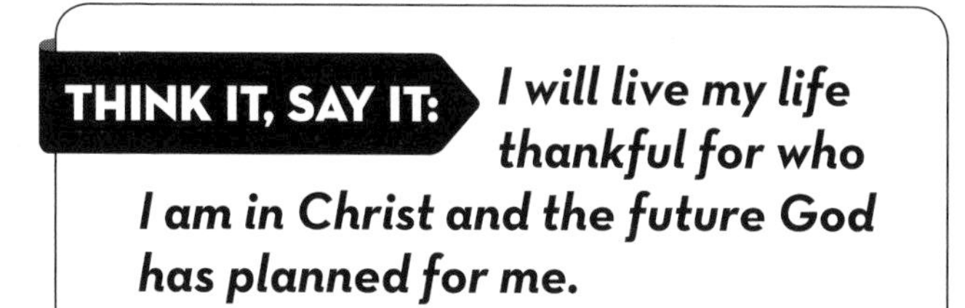

BELIEVE IT:

Thank [God] in everything [no matter what the circumstances may be, be thankful and give thanks], for this is the will of God for you [who are] in Christ Jesus [the Revealer and Mediator of that will].
1 THESSALONIANS 5:18

O give thanks to the Lord, for He is good; for His mercy and loving-kindness endure forever!
PSALM 107:1

Offer to God the sacrifice of thanksgiving, and pay your vows to the Most High,
PSALM 50:14

At all times and for everything giving thanks in the name of our Lord Jesus Christ to God the Father.
EPHESIANS 5:20

Now thanks be to God for His Gift, [precious] beyond telling [His indescribable, inexpressible, free Gift]!
2 CORINTHIANS 9:15

Praise the Lord! (Hallelujah!) O give thanks to the Lord, for He is good; for His mercy and loving-kindness endure forever!

PSALM 106:1

Be earnest and unwearied and steadfast in your prayer [life], being [both] alert and intent in [your praying] with thanksgiving.

COLOSSIANS 4:2

To the end that my tongue and my heart and everything glorious within me may sing praise to You and not be silent. O Lord my God, I will give thanks to You forever.

PSALM 30:12

If possible, as far as it depends on you, live at peace with everyone.

ROMANS 12:18

CHAPTER 3

What am I going to Believe about MY RELATIONSHIPS?

Our relationships are an important part of our lives because they affect so much of what we do. Friends, neighbors, coworkers, family members, and even casual acquaintances are all part of our daily relationships.

The Bible has much to say about how we relate to the people God has put in our lives. When we choose to study God's Word and believe what He says about loving the people around us, our relationships are so much better than when we try to figure things out on our own.

There are unique challenges and demands when dealing with people, but with the help of the Lord, we can meet those challenges with healthy and life-giving results. All we have to do is think, speak and believe what God says about relationships, and walk in love. Then we'll enjoy a brand-new level of peace and contentment in our lives.

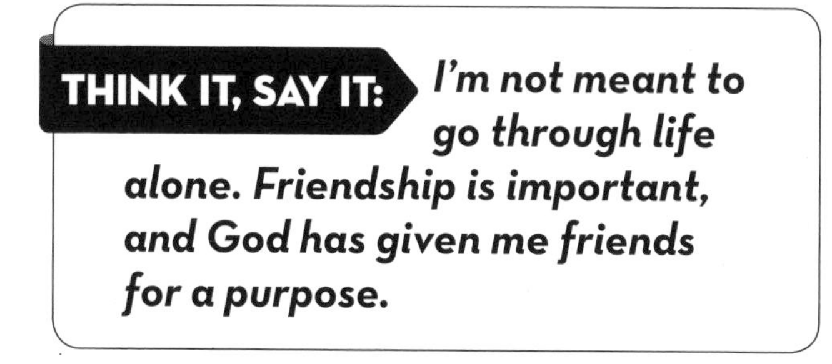

BELIEVE IT:

Two are better than one, because they have a good [more satisfying] reward for their labor; for if they fall, the one will lift up his fellow. But woe to him who is alone when he falls and has not another to lift him up! Again, if two lie down together, then they have warmth; but how can one be warm alone?

ECCLESIASTES 4:9-11

Iron sharpens iron; so a man sharpens the countenance of his friend [to show rage or worthy purpose].

PROVERBS 27:17

A friend loves at all times, and is born, as is a brother, for adversity.

PROVERBS 17:17

Do two walk together except they make an appointment and have agreed?

AMOS 3:3

No one has greater love [no one has shown stronger affection] than to lay down (give up) his own life for his friends.

JOHN 15:13

Oil and perfume rejoice the heart; so does the sweetness of a friend's counsel that comes from the heart.

PROVERBS 27:9

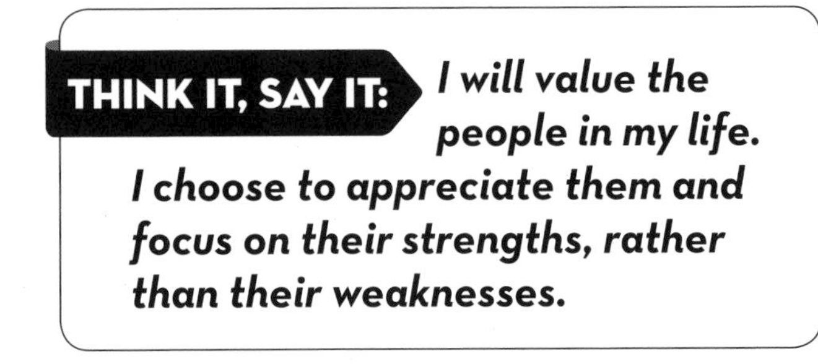

BELIEVE IT:

Your own friend and your father's friend, forsake them not; neither go to your brother's house in the day of your calamity. Better is a neighbor who is near [in spirit] than a brother who is far off [in heart].

PROVERBS 27:10

And though a man might prevail against him who is alone, two will withstand him. A threefold cord is not quickly broken.

ECCLESIASTES 4:12

And let us consider and give attentive, continuous care to watching over one another, studying how we may stir up (stimulate and incite) to love and helpful deeds and noble activities, not forsaking or neglecting to assemble together [as believers], as is the habit of some people, but admonishing (warning, urging, and encouraging) one another, and all the more faithfully as you see the day approaching.

HEBREWS 10:24-25

Above all things have intense and unfailing love for one another, for love covers a multitude of sins [forgives and disregards the offenses of others].

1 PETER 4:8

Faithful are the wounds of a friend, but the kisses of an enemy are lavish and deceitful.

PROVERBS 27:6

Love is patient, love is kind. It does not envy, it does not boast, it is not proud. It does not dishonor others, it is not self-seeking, it is not easily angered, it keeps no record of wrongs. Love does not delight in evil but rejoices with the truth. It always protects, always trusts, always hopes, always perseveres.

1 CORINTHIANS 13:4-7 NIV

The man of many friends [a friend of all the world] will prove himself a bad friend, but there is a friend who sticks closer than a brother.

PROVERBS 18:24

Today, instead of stress or turmoil, I will find joy in the relationships God has given me.

BELIEVE IT:

I have great boldness and free and fearless confidence and cheerful courage toward you; my pride in you is great. I am filled [brimful] with the comfort [of it]; with all our tribulation and in spite of it, [I am filled with comfort] I am overflowing with joy.

2 CORINTHIANS 7:4

So that by God's will I may subsequently come to you with joy (with a happy heart) and be refreshed [by the interval of rest] in your company.

ROMANS 15:32

I have many things to write to you, but I prefer not to do so with paper and ink; I hope to come to see you and talk with you face to face, so that our joy may be complete.

2 JOHN 1:12

Not that we have dominion [over you] and lord it over your faith, but [rather that we work with you as] fellow laborers [to promote] your joy, for in [your] faith (in your strong and welcome conviction or belief that Jesus is the Messiah, through Whom we obtain eternal salvation in the kingdom of God) you stand firm.
2 CORINTHIANS 1:24

And we are now writing these things to you so that our joy [in seeing you included] may be full [and your joy may be complete].
1 JOHN 1:4

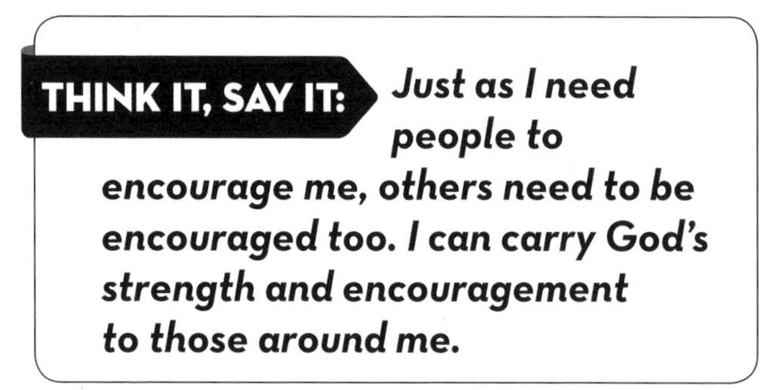

BELIEVE IT:

. . . Encourage the timid and fainthearted, help and give your support to the weak souls, [and] be very patient with everybody [always keeping your temper].
1 THESSALONIANS 5:14

Therefore encourage (admonish, exhort) one another and edify (strengthen and build up) one another, just as you are doing.
1 THESSALONIANS 5:11

For I am yearning to see you, that I may impart and share with you some spiritual gift to strengthen and establish you; that is, that we may be mutually strengthened and encouraged and comforted by each other's faith, both yours and mine.
ROMANS 1:11-12

Let the word [spoken by] Christ (the Messiah) have its home [in your hearts and minds] and dwell in you in [all its] richness, as you teach and admonish and train one another in all insight and intelligence and wisdom [in spiritual things, and as you sing] psalms and hymns and spiritual songs, making melody to God with [His] grace in your hearts.
COLOSSIANS 3:16

Herald and preach the Word! Keep your sense of urgency [stand by, be at hand and ready], whether the opportunity seems to be favorable or unfavorable. [Whether it is convenient or inconvenient, whether it is welcome or unwelcome, you as preacher of the Word are to show people in what way their lives are wrong.] And convince them, rebuking and correcting, warning and urging and encouraging them, being unflagging and inexhaustible in patience and teaching.
2 TIMOTHY 4:2

The mouth of the [uncompromisingly] righteous man is a well of life . . . .
PROVERBS 10:11

Then we, the living ones who remain [on the earth], shall simultaneously be caught up along with [the resurrected dead] in the clouds to meet the Lord in the air; and so always (through the eternity of the eternities) we shall be with the Lord! Therefore comfort and encourage one another with these words.
1 THESSALONIANS 4:17-18

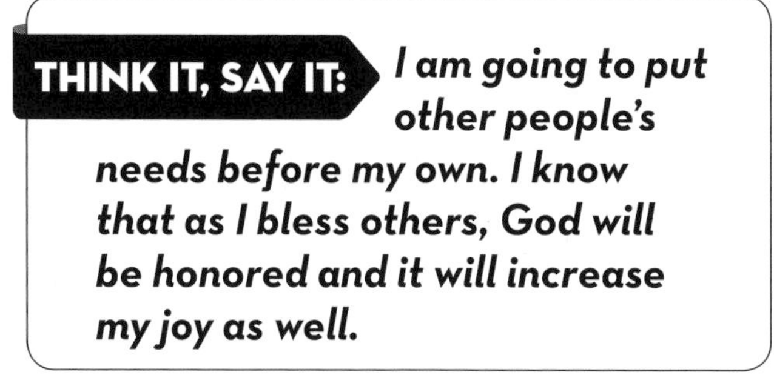

BELIEVE IT:

But instead warn (admonish, urge, and encourage) one another every day, as long as it is called Today, that none of you may be hardened [into settled rebellion] by the deceitfulness of sin [by the fraudulence, the stratagem, the trickery which the delusive glamor of his sin may play on him].
HEBREWS 3:13

She comforts, encourages, and does him only good as long as there is life within her.

PROVERBS 31:12

But God, Who comforts and encourages and refreshes and cheers the depressed and the sinking, comforted and encouraged and refreshed and cheered us by the arrival of Titus.

2 CORINTHIANS 7:6

Anxiety in a man's heart weighs it down, but an encouraging word makes it glad.

PROVERBS 12:25

For you know how, as a father [dealing with] his children, we used to exhort each of you personally, stimulating and encouraging and charging you to live lives worthy of God, Who calls you into His own kingdom and the glorious blessedness [into which true believers will enter after Christ's return].

1 THESSALONIANS 2:11-12

I have sent him to you for this very purpose, that you may know how we are and that he may console and cheer and encourage and strengthen your hearts.

EPHESIANS 6:22

So [Paul and Silas] left the prison and went to Lydia's house; and when they had seen the brethren, they warned and urged and consoled and encouraged them and departed.

ACTS 16:40

So [instead of further rebuke, now] you should rather turn and [graciously] forgive and comfort and encourage [him], to keep him from being overwhelmed by excessive sorrow and despair.

2 CORINTHIANS 2:7

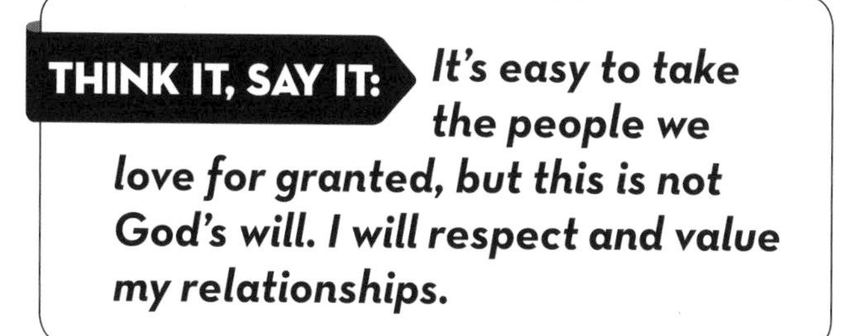

BELIEVE IT:

Practice hospitality to one another (those of the household of faith). [Be hospitable, be a lover of strangers, with brotherly affection for the unknown guests, the foreigners, the poor, and all others who come your way who are of Christ's body.] And [in each instance] do it ungrudgingly (cordially and graciously, without complaining but as representing Him).

1 PETER 4:9

Bear (endure, carry) one another's burdens and troublesome moral faults, and in this way fulfill and observe perfectly the law of Christ (the Messiah) and complete what is lacking [in your obedience to it].

GALATIANS 6:2

To him who is about to faint and despair, kindness is due from his friend, lest he forsake the fear of the Almighty.

JOB 6:14

A soft answer turns away wrath, but grievous words stir up anger.

PROVERBS 15:1

And David said, Is there still anyone left of the house of Saul to whom I may show kindness for Jonathan's sake?

2 SAMUEL 9:1

And as you would like and desire that men would do to you, do exactly so to them.

LUKE 6:31

David said, I will show kindness to Hanun son of Nahash, as his father did to me . . . .

2 SAMUEL 10:2

Love one another with brotherly affection [as members of one family], giving precedence and showing honor to one another.

ROMANS 12:10

Render to all men their dues . . . respect to whom respect is due, and honor to whom honor is due.

ROMANS 13:7

Unity is important to me because it is important to God. I will not be divisive — I will be a peacemaker.

BELIEVE IT:

Behold, how good and how pleasant it is for brethren to dwell together in unity!

PSALM 133:1

Be eager and strive earnestly to guard and keep the harmony and oneness of [and produced by] the Spirit in the binding power of peace.

EPHESIANS 4:3

But I urge and entreat you, brethren, by the name of our Lord Jesus Christ, that all of you be in perfect harmony and full agreement in what you say, and that there be no dissensions or factions or divisions among you, but that you be perfectly united in your common understanding and in your opinions and judgments.

1 CORINTHIANS 1:10

For wherever two or three are gathered (drawn together as My followers) in (into) My name, there I AM in the midst of them.

MATTHEW 18:20

He who covers and forgives an offense seeks love, but he who repeats or harps on a matter separates even close friends.

PROVERBS 17:9

Fill up and complete my joy by living in harmony and being of the same mind and one in purpose, having the same love, being in full accord and of one harmonious mind and intention.

PHILIPPIANS 2:2

Finally, all [of you] should be of one and the same mind (united in spirit), sympathizing [with one another], loving [each other] as brethren [of one household], compassionate and courteous (tender-hearted and humble).

1 PETER 3:8

Finally, brethren, farewell (rejoice)! Be strengthened (perfected, completed, made what you ought to be); be encouraged and consoled and comforted; be of the same [agreeable] mind one with another; live in peace, and [then] the God of love [Who is the Source of affection, goodwill, love, and benevolence toward men] and the Author and Promoter of peace will be with you.

2 CORINTHIANS 13:11

That together you may [unanimously] with united hearts and one voice, praise and glorify the God and Father of our Lord Jesus Christ (the Messiah).

ROMANS 15:6

Only be sure as citizens so to conduct yourselves [that] your manner of life [will be] worthy of the good news (the Gospel) of Christ, so that whether I [do] come and see you or am absent, I may hear this of you: that you are standing firm in united spirit and purpose, striving side by side and contending with a single mind for the faith of the glad tidings (the Gospel).

PHILIPPIANS 1:27

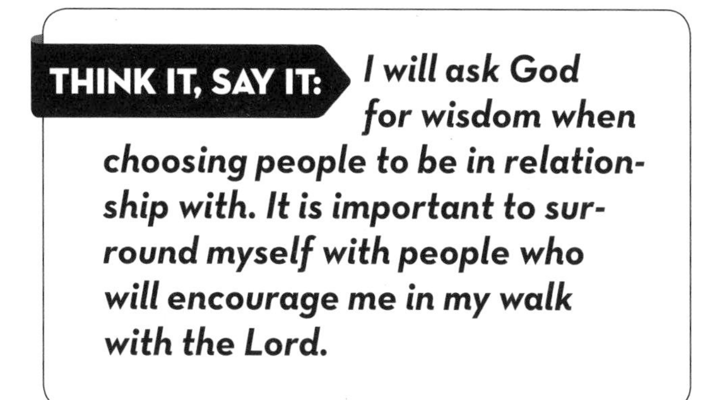

THINK IT, SAY IT: ***I will ask God for wisdom when choosing people to be in relationship with. It is important to surround myself with people who will encourage me in my walk with the Lord.***

BELIEVE IT:

Do not be so deceived and misled! Evil companionships (communion, associations) corrupt and deprave good manners and morals and character.

1 CORINTHIANS 15:33

Confidence in an unfaithful man in time of trouble is like a broken tooth or a foot out of joint.

PROVERBS 25:19

As in water face answers to and reflects face, so the heart of man to man.

PROVERBS 27:19

A perverse man sows strife, and a whisperer separates close friends.

PROVERBS 16:28

Even my own familiar friend, in whom I trusted (relied on and was confident), who ate of my bread, has lifted up his heel against me.

PSALM 41:9

. . . Do you not know that being the world's friend is being God's enemy? So whoever chooses to be a friend of the world takes his stand as an enemy of God.

JAMES 4:4

Make no friendships with a man given to anger, and with a wrathful man do not associate, lest you learn his ways and get yourself into a snare.

PROVERBS 22:24-25

Two are better than one, because they have a good [more satisfying] reward for their labor; for if they fall, the one will lift up his fellow. But woe to him who is alone when he falls and has not another to lift him up!

ECCLESIASTES 4:9-10

THINK IT, SAY IT: ***When someone hurts or offends me, I am called to forgive just as God has forgiven me.***

BELIEVE IT:

And become useful and helpful and kind to one another, tenderhearted (compassionate, understanding, loving-hearted), forgiving one another [readily and freely], as God in Christ forgave you.

EPHESIANS 4:32

Pay attention and always be on your guard [looking out for one another]. If your brother sins (misses the mark), solemnly tell him so and reprove him, and if he repents (feels sorry for having sinned), forgive him. And even if he sins against you seven times in a day, and turns to you seven times and says, I repent [I am sorry], you must forgive him (give up resentment and consider the offense as recalled and annulled).

LUKE 17:3-4

Confess to one another therefore your faults (your slips, your false steps, your offenses, your sins) and pray [also] for one another, that you may be healed and restored [to a spiritual tone of mind and heart]....

JAMES 5:16

And whenever you stand praying, if you have anything against anyone, forgive him and let it drop (leave it, let it go), in order that your Father Who is in heaven may also forgive you your [own] failings and shortcomings and let them drop.

MARK 11:25

Be gentle and forbearing with one another and, if one has a difference (a grievance or complaint) against another, readily pardoning each other; even as the Lord has [freely] forgiven you, so must you also [forgive].

COLOSSIANS 3:13

Judge not [neither pronouncing judgment nor subjecting to censure], and you will not be judged; do not condemn and pronounce guilty, and you will not be condemned and pronounced guilty; acquit and forgive and release (give up resentment, let it drop), and you will be acquitted and forgiven and released.

LUKE 6:37

Never return evil for evil or insult for insult (scolding, tongue-lashing, berating), but on the contrary blessing [praying for their welfare, happiness, and protection, and truly pitying and loving them]. For know that to this you have been called, that you may yourselves inherit a blessing [from God—that you may obtain a blessing as heirs, bringing welfare and happiness and protection].

1 PETER 3:9

And Jesus prayed, Father, forgive them, for they know not what they do . . . .

LUKE 23:34

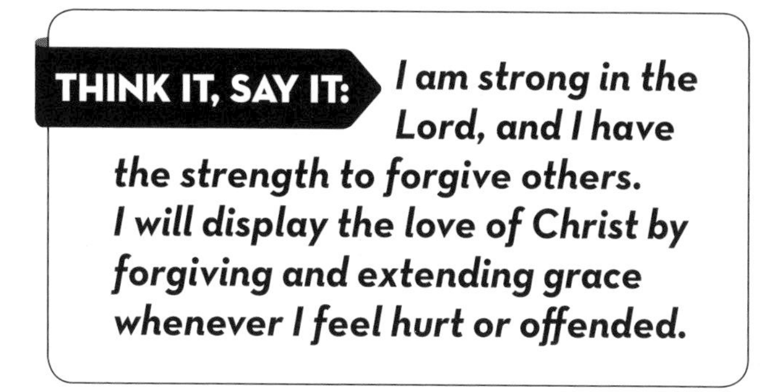

BELIEVE IT:

If possible, as far as it depends on you, live at peace with everyone.

ROMANS 12:18

And forgive us our debts, as we also have forgiven (left, remitted, and let go of the debts, and have given up resentment against) our debtors.

MATTHEW 6:12

So if when you are offering your gift at the altar you there remember that your brother has any [grievance] against you, leave your gift at the altar and go. First make peace with your brother, and then come back and present your gift.

MATTHEW 5:23-24

A hot-tempered man stirs up strife, but he who is slow to anger appeases contention.

PROVERBS 15:18

Blessed (enjoying enviable happiness, spiritually prosperous—with life-joy and satisfaction in God's favor and salvation, regardless of their outward conditions) are the makers and maintainers of peace, for they shall be called the sons of God!

MATTHEW 5:9

. . . Be at peace among yourselves.

1 THESSALONIANS 5:13

. . . Walk (lead a life) worthy of the [divine] calling to which you have been called [with behavior that is a credit to the summons to God's service.

EPHESIANS 4:1

Beloved, never avenge yourselves, but leave the way open for [God's] wrath; for it is written, Vengeance is Mine, I will repay (requite), says the Lord.

ROMANS 12:19

Then Peter came up to Him and said, Lord, how many times may my brother sin against me and I forgive him and let it go? [As many as] up to seven times? Jesus answered him, I tell you, not up to seven times, but seventy times seven!

MATTHEW 18:21-22

THINK IT, SAY IT: ***I choose to live a life of love and I'm going to share the love of God with all those around me.***

BELIEVE IT:

This is My commandment: that you love one another [just] as I have loved you.

JOHN 15:12

Let all bitterness and indignation and wrath (passion, rage, bad temper) and resentment (anger, animosity) and quarreling (brawling, clamor, contention) and slander (evil-speaking, abusive or blasphemous language) be banished from you, with all malice (spite, ill will, or baseness of any kind).

EPHESIANS 4:31

If I [can] speak in the tongues of men and [even] of angels, but have not love (that reasoning, intentional, spiritual devotion such as is inspired by God's love for and in us), I am only a noisy gong or a clanging cymbal.

1 CORINTHIANS 13:1

He loves righteousness and justice; the earth is full of the loving-kindness of the Lord.

PSALM 33:5

Beloved, let us love one another, for love is (springs) from God; and he who loves [his fellowmen] is begotten (born) of God and is coming [progressively] to know and understand God [to perceive and recognize and get a better and clearer knowledge of Him].

1 JOHN 4:7

Above all things have intense and unfailing love for one another, for love covers a multitude of sins [forgives and disregards the offenses of others].

1 PETER 4:8

And above all these [put on] love and enfold yourselves with the bond of perfectness [which binds everything together completely in ideal harmony].

COLOSSIANS 3:14

If you [merely] love those who love you, what quality of credit and thanks is that to you? For even the [very] sinners love their lovers (those who love them).

LUKE 6:32

I have loved you, [just] as the Father has loved Me; abide in My love [continue in His love with Me].

JOHN 15:9

In this the love of God was made manifest (displayed) where we are concerned: in that God sent His Son, the only begotten or unique [Son], into the world so that we might live through Him.

1 JOHN 4:9

Even while I am dealing with relationship issues, I will keep God number one in my life. My relationship with Him is the most important one I have.

BELIEVE IT:

And He replied to him, You shall love the Lord your God with all your heart and with all your soul and with all your mind (intellect). This is the great (most important, principal) and first commandment.

MATTHEW 22:37-38

If then you have been raised with Christ [to a new life, thus sharing His resurrection from the dead], aim at and seek the [rich, eternal treasures] that are above, where Christ is, seated at the right hand of God. And set your minds and keep them set on what is above (the higher things), not on the things that are on the earth.

COLOSSIANS 3:1-2

But God shows and clearly proves His [own] love for us by the fact that while we were still sinners, Christ (the Messiah, the Anointed One) died for us.

ROMANS 5:8

For the Lord your God is a consuming fire, a jealous God.
DEUTERONOMY 4:24

The Lord is good to those who wait hopefully and expectantly for Him, to those who seek Him [inquire of and for Him and require Him by right of necessity and on the authority of God's word].
LAMENTATIONS 3:25

For those who are according to the flesh and are controlled by its unholy desires set their minds on and pursue those things which gratify the flesh, but those who are according to the Spirit and are controlled by the desires of the Spirit set their minds on and seek those things which gratify the [Holy] Spirit.
ROMANS 8:5

Have not I commanded you? Be strong, vigorous, and very courageous. Be not afraid, neither be dismayed, for the Lord your God is with you wherever you go.

JOSHUA 1:9

CHAPTER 4

What am I going to Believe about MY LIFE?

God created you to live an abundant, overflowing, joy-filled life in Him. You aren't meant to go through life depressed or defeated. Jesus died so you could live an overcoming, victorious life—a life that you can enjoy every day.

Too many times we go through each day with a "survivor mentality." We think: *If I can just survive this day* . . . or *If I can just make it through one more day* . . . but this isn't God's plan for your life. God's plan and purposes for your life are greater than anything you could even imagine.

Instead of just surviving each day, believe that with the help of the Holy Spirit, you can thrive each day. Line your thoughts, words and actions up with the Word of God and begin living the overcoming, abundant, joy-filled life that has been given to you in Christ Jesus.

I am created by God to live a life full of joy and happiness.

BELIEVE IT:

The thief comes only in order to steal and kill and destroy. I came that they may have and enjoy life, and have it in abundance (to the full, till it overflows).
JOHN 10:10

And now I am coming to You; I say these things while I am still in the world, so that My joy may be made full and complete and perfect in them [that they may experience My delight fulfilled in them, that My enjoyment may be perfected in their own souls, that they may have My gladness within them, filling their hearts].
JOHN 17:13

For you shall go out [from the spiritual exile caused by sin and evil into the homeland] with joy and be led forth [by your Leader, the Lord Himself, and His word] with peace; the mountains and the hills shall break forth before you into singing, and all the trees of the field shall clap their hands.
ISAIAH 55:12

Up to this time you have not asked a [single] thing in My Name [as presenting all that I Am]; but now ask and keep on asking and you will receive, so that your joy (gladness, delight) may be full and complete.
JOHN 16:24

The hope of the [uncompromisingly] righteous (the upright, in right standing with God) is gladness . . . .
PROVERBS 10:28

[We pray] that you may be invigorated and strengthened with all power according to the might of His glory, [to exercise] every kind of endurance and patience (perseverance and forbearance) with joy.
COLOSSIANS 1:11

Make a joyful noise to the Lord, all you lands! Serve the Lord with gladness! Come before His presence with singing!
PSALM 100:1-2

Now to Him Who is able to keep you without stumbling or slipping or falling, and to present [you] unblemished (blameless and faultless) before the presence of His glory in triumphant joy and exultation [with unspeakable, ecstatic delight].
JUDE 1:24

Yes, if a man should live many years, let him rejoice in them all . . . .
ECCLESIASTES 11:8

THINK IT, SAY IT: ***I am strong because the joy of the Lord is my strength.***

BELIEVE IT:

. . . And be not grieved and depressed, for the joy of the Lord is your strength and stronghold.
NEHEMIAH 8:10

My lips shall shout for joy when I sing praises to You, and my inner being, which You have redeemed.
PSALM 71:23

You will show me the path of life; in Your presence is fullness of joy, at Your right hand there are pleasures forevermore.
PSALM 16:11

For to the person who pleases Him God gives wisdom and knowledge and joy . . . .
ECCLESIASTES 2:26

His master said to him, Well done, you upright (honorable, admirable) and faithful servant! You have been faithful and trustworthy over a little; I will put you in charge of much. Enter into and share the joy (the delight, the blessedness) which your master enjoys.
MATTHEW 25:21

I have told you these things, that My joy and delight may be in you, and that your joy and gladness may be of full measure and complete and overflowing.
JOHN 15:11

You have made known to me the ways of life; You will enrapture me [diffusing my soul with joy] with and in Your presence.
ACTS 2:28

And the disciples were continually filled [throughout their souls] with joy and the Holy Spirit.
ACTS 13:52

And He brought forth His people with joy, and His chosen ones with gladness and singing.
PSALM 105:43

Laughter is a good medicine—today I'm going to look for opportunities to laugh and enjoy the life God has given me.

BELIEVE IT:

A glad heart makes a cheerful countenance, but by sorrow of heart the spirit is broken.
PROVERBS 15:13

Then were our mouths filled with laughter, and our tongues with singing. Then they said among the nations, The Lord has done great things for them.
PSALM 126:2

He will yet fill your mouth with laughter [Job] and your lips with joyful shouting.
JOB 8:21

A time to weep and a time to laugh, a time to mourn and a time to dance.
ECCLESIASTES 3:4

He Who sits in the heavens laughs . . . .
PSALM 2:4

And Sarah said, God has made me to laugh; all who hear will laugh with me.
GENESIS 21:6

The Lord laughs at [the wicked], for He sees that their own day [of defeat] is coming.
PSALM 37:13

For You have been my help, and in the shadow of Your wings will I rejoice.
PSALM 63:7

In Your name they rejoice all the day, and in Your righteousness they are exalted.
PSALM 89:16

God is bigger than any fear I might face, and I can trust Him to deliver me from my fears.

BELIEVE IT:

What time I am afraid, I will have confidence in and put my trust and reliance in You. By [the help of] God I will praise His word; on God I lean, rely, and confidently put my trust; I will not fear. What can man, who is flesh, do to me?

PSALM 56:3-4

There is no fear in love [dread does not exist], but full-grown (complete, perfect) love turns fear out of doors and expels every trace of terror! For fear brings with it the thought of punishment, and [so] he who is afraid has not reached the full maturity of love [is not yet grown into love's complete perfection].

1 JOHN 4:18

So we take comfort and are encouraged and confidently and boldly say, The Lord is my Helper; I will not be seized with alarm [I will not fear or dread or be terrified]. What can man do to me?

HEBREWS 13:6

Have not I commanded you? Be strong, vigorous, and very courageous. Be not afraid, neither be dismayed, for the Lord your God is with you wherever you go.
JOSHUA 1:9

Fret not yourself because of evildoers, neither be envious against those who work unrighteousness (that which is not upright or in right standing with God).
PSALM 37:1

So have no fear of them; for nothing is concealed that will not be revealed, or kept secret that will not become known.
MATTHEW 10:26

The Lord is my Light and my Salvation—whom shall I fear or dread? The Lord is the Refuge and Stronghold of my life—of whom shall I be afraid?
PSALM 27:1

Now may the Lord of peace Himself grant you His peace (the peace of His kingdom) at all times and in all ways [under all circumstances and conditions, whatever comes]. The Lord [be] with you all.
2 THESSALONIANS 3:16

Then they cried to the Lord in their trouble, and He delivered them out of their distresses.
PSALM 107:6

THINK IT, SAY IT: ***I will not shrink back in fear even when I feel afraid. Instead, I will press forward and enjoy my life.***

BELIEVE IT:

Overhearing but ignoring what they said, Jesus said to the ruler of the synagogue, Do not be seized with alarm and struck with fear; only keep on believing.
MARK 5:36

Then I said to you, Dread not, neither be afraid of them. The Lord your God Who goes before you, He will fight for you just as He did for you in Egypt before your eyes.
DEUTERONOMY 1:29-30

And do not [for a moment] be frightened or intimidated in anything by your opponents and adversaries, for such [constancy and fearlessness] will be a clear sign (proof and seal) to them of [their impending] destruction, but [a sure token and evidence] of your deliverance and salvation, and that from God.
PHILIPPIANS 1:28

. . . Be strong and of good courage. Dread not and fear not; be not dismayed.
1 CHRONICLES 22:13

He shall not be afraid of evil tidings; his heart is firmly fixed, trusting (leaning on and being confident) in the Lord.

PSALM 112:7

Also David told Solomon his son, Be strong and courageous, and do it. Fear not, be not dismayed, for the Lord God, my God, is with you. He will not fail or forsake you until you have finished all the work for the service of the house of the Lord.

1 CHRONICLES 28:20

But instantly He spoke to them, saying, Take courage! I Am! Stop being afraid!

MATTHEW 14:27

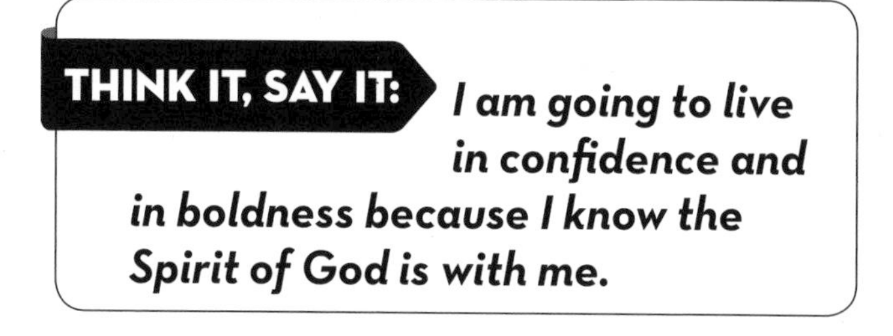

BELIEVE IT:

And when they had prayed, the place in which they were assembled was shaken; and they were all filled with the Holy Spirit, and they continued to speak the Word of God with freedom and boldness and courage.

ACTS 4:31

In Whom, because of our faith in Him, we dare to have the boldness (courage and confidence) of free access (an unreserved approach to God with freedom and without fear).

EPHESIANS 3:12

Since we have such [glorious] hope (such joyful and confident expectation), we speak very freely and openly and fearlessly.

2 CORINTHIANS 3:12

Preaching to them the kingdom of God and teaching them about the Lord Jesus Christ with boldness and quite openly . . . .

ACTS 28:31

The wicked flee when no man pursues them, but the [uncompromisingly] righteous are bold as a lion.

PROVERBS 28:1

Now when they saw the boldness and unfettered eloquence of Peter and John and perceived that they were unlearned and untrained in the schools [common men with no educational advantages], they marveled; and they recognized that they had been with Jesus.

ACTS 4:13

And now, Lord, observe their threats and grant to Your bond servants [full freedom] to declare Your message fearlessly.

ACTS 4:29

THINK IT, SAY IT: ***No matter how difficult the circumstance may seem, the joy of the Lord is my strength.***

BELIEVE IT:

. . . With all our tribulation and in spite of it, [I am filled with comfort] I am overflowing with joy.

2 CORINTHIANS 7:4

So for the present you are also in sorrow (in distress and depressed); but I will see you again and [then] your hearts will rejoice, and no one can take from you your joy (gladness, delight).

JOHN 16:22

But insofar as you are sharing Christ's sufferings, rejoice, so that when His glory [full of radiance and splendor] is revealed, you may also rejoice with triumph [exultantly].

1 PETER 4:13

For in the midst of an ordeal of severe tribulation, their abundance of joy and their depth of poverty [together] have overflowed in wealth of lavish generosity on their part.

2 CORINTHIANS 8:2

Consider it wholly joyful, my brethren, whenever you are enveloped in or encounter trials of any sort or fall into various temptations. Be assured and understand that the trial and proving of your faith bring out endurance and steadfastness and patience. But let endurance and steadfastness and patience have full play and do a thorough work, so that you may be [people] perfectly and fully developed [with no defects], lacking in nothing.

JAMES 1:2-4

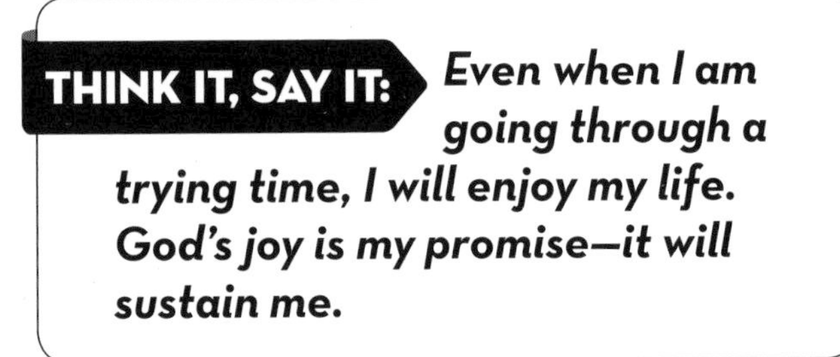

BELIEVE IT:

. . . Weeping may endure for a night, but joy comes in the morning.

PSALM 30:5

And you [set yourselves to] become imitators of us and [through us] of the Lord Himself, for you welcomed our message in [spite of] much persecution, with joy [inspired] by the Holy Spirit.

1 THESSALONIANS 1:6

I have told you these things, so that in Me you may have [perfect] peace and confidence. In the world you have tribulation and trials and distress and frustration; but be of good cheer [take courage; be confident, certain, undaunted]! For I have overcome the world. [I have deprived it of power to harm you and have conquered it for you.]

JOHN 16:33

They who sow in tears shall reap in joy and singing.

PSALM 126:5

He who goes forth bearing seed and weeping [at needing his precious supply of grain for sowing] shall doubtless come again with rejoicing, bringing his sheaves with him.

PSALM 126:6

Looking away [from all that will distract] to Jesus, Who is the Leader and the Source of our faith [giving the first incentive for our belief] and is also its Finisher [bringing it to maturity and perfection]. He, for the joy [of obtaining the prize] that was set before Him, endured the cross, despising and ignoring the shame, and is now seated at the right hand of the throne of God.

HEBREWS 12:2

I lay down and slept; I wakened again, for the Lord sustains me.

PSALM 3:5

All throughout the day, I am going to take time to rejoice in the Lord.

BELIEVE IT:

Rejoice in the Lord always [delight, gladden yourselves in Him]; again I say, Rejoice!

PHILIPPIANS 4:4

Therefore my heart is glad and my glory [my inner self] rejoices; my body too shall rest and confidently dwell in safety.

PSALM 16:9

Be happy [in your faith] and rejoice and be glad-hearted continually (always).

1 THESSALONIANS 5:16

Not only so, but we also rejoice and exultingly glory in God [in His love and perfection] through our Lord Jesus Christ, through Whom we have now received and enjoy [our] reconciliation.

ROMANS 5:11

This is the day which the Lord has brought about; we will rejoice and be glad in it.

PSALM 118:24

For in Him does our heart rejoice, because we have trusted (relied on and been confident) in His holy name.

PSALM 33:21

You have put more joy and rejoicing in my heart than [they know] . . . .

PSALM 4:7

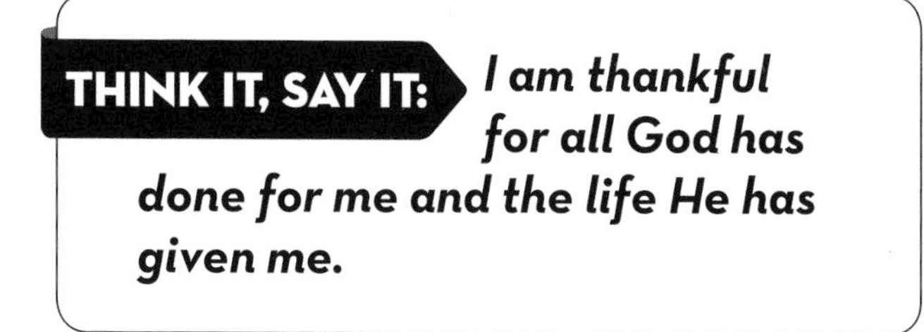

BELIEVE IT:

. . . Great and abundant is Your stability and faithfulness.

LAMENTATIONS 3:23

I will give to the Lord the thanks due to His rightness and justice, and I will sing praise to the name of the Lord Most High.

PSALM 7:17

Bless (affectionately, gratefully praise) the Lord, O my soul, and forget not [one of] all His benefits.

PSALM 103:2

Every good gift and every perfect (free, large, full) gift is from above; it comes down from the Father of all [that gives] light, in [the shining of] Whom there can be no variation [rising or setting] or shadow cast by His turning [as in an eclipse].

JAMES 1:17

. . . And be thankful (appreciative), [giving praise to God always].

COLOSSIANS 3:15

We give praise and thanks to You, O God, we praise and give thanks; Your wondrous works declare that Your Name is near and they who invoke Your Name rehearse Your wonders.

PSALM 75:1

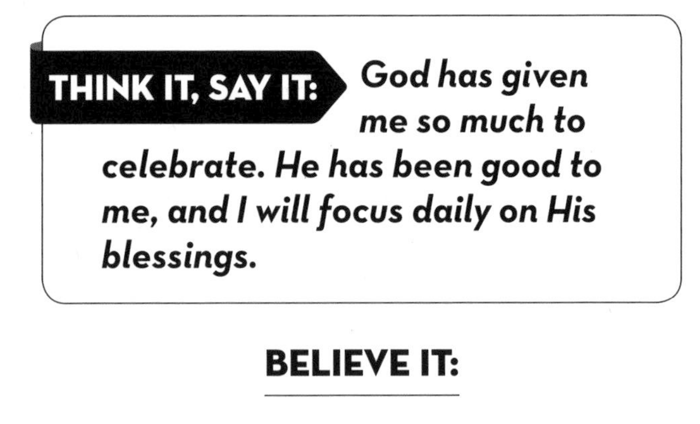

BELIEVE IT:

Sing and rejoice, O Daughter of Zion; for behold, I come, and I will dwell in the midst of you, says the Lord.

ZECHARIAH 2:10

The Lord is my Strength and my [impenetrable] Shield; my heart trusts in, relies on, and confidently leans on Him, and I am helped; therefore my heart greatly rejoices, and with my song will I praise Him.
PSALM 28:7

And my spirit rejoices in God my Savior.
LUKE 1:47

Also that day they offered great sacrifices and rejoiced, for God had made them rejoice with great joy; the women also and the children rejoiced. The joy of Jerusalem was heard even afar off.
NEHEMIAH 12:43

May all those who seek, inquire of and for You, and require You [as their vital need] rejoice and be glad in You; and may those who love Your salvation say continually, Let God be magnified!
PSALM 70:4

May my meditation be sweet to Him; as for me, I will rejoice in the Lord.
PSALM 104:34

Fear not, O land; be glad and rejoice, for the Lord has done great things!
JOEL 2:21

In Your name they rejoice all the day, and in Your righteousness they are exalted.
PSALM 89:16

I can enjoy my life because I have an intimate, personal relationship with God. I will delight in Him.

BELIEVE IT:

Delight yourself also in the Lord, and He will give you the desires and secret petitions of your heart.
PSALM 37:4

Then will you delight yourself in the Lord, and I will make you to ride on the high places of the earth, and I will feed you with the heritage [promised for you] of Jacob your father; for the mouth of the Lord has spoken it.
ISAIAH 58:14

Then you will have delight in the Almighty, and you will lift up your face to God.
JOB 22:26

The king [David] shall joy in Your strength, O Lord; and in Your salvation how greatly shall he rejoice! You have given him his heart's desire and have not withheld the request of his lips. Selah [pause, and think of that]!
PSALM 21:1-2

May my meditation be sweet to Him; as for me, I will rejoice in the Lord.

PSALM 104:34

Then will I go to the altar of God, to God, my exceeding joy; yes, with the lyre will I praise You, O God, my God!

PSALM 43:4

The precepts of the Lord are right, rejoicing the heart; the commandment of the Lord is pure and bright, enlightening the eyes.

PSALM 19:8

But the meek [in the end] shall inherit the earth and shall delight themselves in the abundance of peace.

PSALM 37:11

How sweet are Your words to my taste, sweeter than honey to my mouth!

PSALM 119:103

Open my eyes, that I may behold wondrous things out of Your law.

PSALM 119:18

He brought me forth into a large place; He delivered me because He delighted in me.

2 SAMUEL 22:20

And there is hope for your future, says the Lord . . . .

JEREMIAH 31:17

CHAPTER 5

What am I going to Believe about MY FUTURE?

Every person who belongs to the family of God has a great future ahead of them. We can be filled with hope and anticipation because we know God is with us, and He has a wonderful plan for our lives.

Many people put their trust in external and temporary things. They think a job, an investment, an industry or even a relationship is the key to their future happiness. God can certainly use these things to bring blessings into our lives, but He alone should be the foundation for our hope and trust.

As you look ahead to the days and years to come, believe what God says about your future in Him. Stand firm on His promises, knowing His plans will come to pass in your life.

I can expect a good future because I have the hope of God's promises.

BELIEVE IT:

For surely there is a latter end [a future and a reward], and your hope and expectation shall not be cut off.

PROVERBS 23:18

But if we hope for what is still unseen by us, we wait for it with patience and composure.

ROMANS 8:25

Hope deferred makes the heart sick, but when the desire is fulfilled, it is a tree of life.

PROVERBS 13:12

Because of the hope [of experiencing what is] laid up (reserved and waiting) for you in heaven. Of this [hope] you heard in the past in the message of the truth of the Gospel.

COLOSSIANS 1:5

For in You, O Lord, do I hope; You will answer, O Lord my God.

PSALM 38:15

O love the Lord, all you His saints! The Lord preserves the faithful, and plentifully pays back him who deals haughtily. Be strong and let your heart take courage, all you who wait for and hope for and expect the Lord!

PSALM 31:23-24

. . . Commanding our fathers that they should make [the great facts of God's dealings with Israel] known to their children, that the generation to come might know them, that the children still to be born might arise and recount them to their children, that they might set their hope in God and not forget the works of God, but might keep His commandments.

PSALM 78:5-7

[What, what would have become of me] had I not believed that I would see the Lord's goodness in the land of the living! Wait and hope for and expect the Lord; be brave and of good courage and let your heart be stout and enduring. Yes, wait for and hope for and expect the Lord.

PSALM 27:13-14

You are my hiding place and my shield; I hope in Your word.

PSALM 119:114

And there is hope for your future, says the Lord . . . .

JEREMIAH 31:17

I will not be anxious about my future. Instead, I will be filled with anticipation of what God is going to do in my life.

BELIEVE IT:

Uphold me according to Your promise, that I may live; and let me not be put to shame in my hope! Hold me up, that I may be safe and have regard for Your statutes continually!

PSALM 119:116-117

May the God of your hope so fill you with all joy and peace in believing [through the experience of your faith] that by the power of the Holy Spirit you may abound and be overflowing (bubbling over) with hope.

ROMANS 15:13

Those who trust in, lean on, and confidently hope in the Lord are like Mount Zion, which cannot be moved but abides and stands fast forever. As the mountains are round about Jerusalem, so the Lord is round about His people from this time forth and forever.

PSALM 125:1-2

Remember [fervently] the word and promise to Your servant, in which You have caused me to hope. This is my comfort and consolation in my affliction: that Your word has revived me and given me life.

PSALM 119:49-50

A bruised reed He will not break, and a smoldering (dimly burning) wick He will not quench, till He brings justice and a just cause to victory. And in and on His name will the Gentiles (the peoples outside of Israel) set their hopes.

MATTHEW 12:20-21

For evildoers shall be cut off, but those who wait and hope and look for the Lord [in the end] shall inherit the earth.

PSALM 37:9

O Israel, hope in the Lord! For with the Lord there is mercy and loving-kindness, and with Him is plenteous redemption.

PSALM 130:7

It is good that one should hope in and wait quietly for the salvation (the safety and ease) of the Lord.

LAMENTATIONS 3:26

The Lord takes pleasure in those who reverently and worshipfully fear Him, in those who hope in His mercy and loving-kindness.

PSALM 147:11

I choose to think and speak good things about my future. I have a confident expectation that God has good things in store for me and for my family.

BELIEVE IT:

Remember [fervently] the word and promise to Your servant, in which You have caused me to hope.

PSALM 119:49

Through Him also we have [our] access (entrance, introduction) by faith into this grace (state of God's favor) in which we [firmly and safely] stand. And let us rejoice and exult in our hope of experiencing and enjoying the glory of God.

ROMANS 5:2

[Now] we have this [hope] as a sure and steadfast anchor of the soul [it cannot slip and it cannot break down under whoever steps out upon it—a hope] that reaches farther and enters into [the very certainty of the Presence] within the veil.

HEBREWS 6:19

. . . You are my refuge and my hope in the day of evil.

JEREMIAH 17:17

Since we have such [glorious] hope (such joyful and confident expectation), we speak very freely and openly and fearlessly.
2 CORINTHIANS 3:12

And now, Lord, what do I wait for and expect? My hope and expectation are in You.
PSALM 39:7

. . . I will look for and hope in Him.
ISAIAH 8:17

But I will hope continually, and will praise You yet more and more.
PSALM 71:14

Rejoice and exult in hope; be steadfast and patient in suffering and tribulation; be constant in prayer.
ROMANS 12:12

I waited patiently and expectantly for the Lord; and He inclined to me and heard my cry.
PSALM 40:1

Finally, brothers and sisters, whatever is true, whatever is noble, whatever is right, whatever is pure, whatever is lovely, whatever is admirable—if anything is excellent or praiseworthy—think about such things.
PHILIPPIANS 4:8 NIV

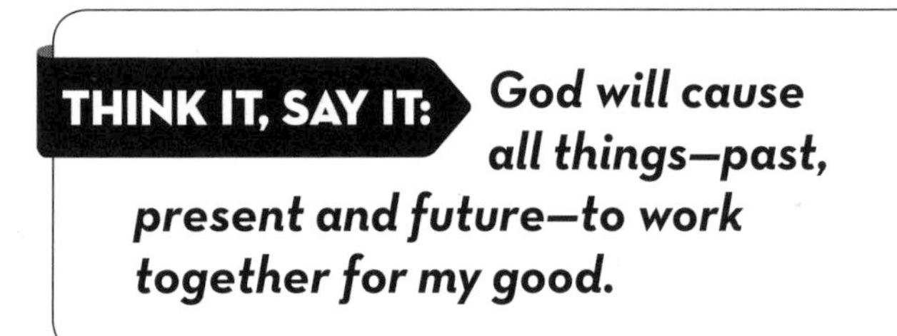

BELIEVE IT:

We are assured and know that [God being a partner in their labor] all things work together and are [fitting into a plan] for good to and for those who love God and are called according to [His] design and purpose.

ROMANS 8:28

Thus says the Lord, your Redeemer, the Holy One of Israel: I am the Lord your God, Who teaches you to profit, Who leads you in the way that you should go.

ISAIAH 48:17

For I know the thoughts and plans that I have for you, says the Lord, thoughts and plans for welfare and peace and not for evil, to give you hope in your final outcome.

JEREMIAH 29:11

A man's mind plans his way, but the Lord directs his steps and makes them sure.

PROVERBS 16:9

Beloved, I pray that you may prosper in every way and [that your body] may keep well, even as [I know] your soul keeps well and prospers.
3 JOHN 1:2

Commit your way to the Lord [roll and repose each care of your load on Him]; trust (lean on, rely on, and be confident) also in Him and He will bring it to pass.
PSALM 37:5

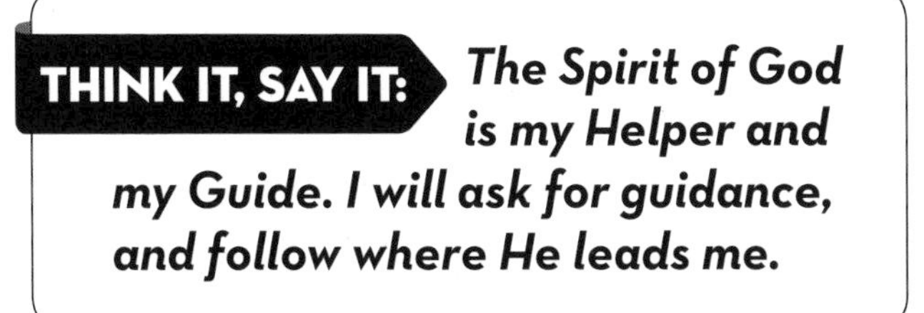

BELIEVE IT:

Show me Your ways, O Lord; teach me Your paths. Guide me in Your truth and faithfulness and teach me, for You are the God of my salvation; for You [You only and altogether] do I wait [expectantly] all the day long.
PSALM 25:4-5

You in Your mercy and loving-kindness have led forth the people whom You have redeemed; You have guided them in Your strength to Your holy habitation.
EXODUS 15:13

And what this love consists in is this: that we live and walk in accordance with and guided by His commandments (His orders, ordinances, precepts, teaching). This is the commandment, as you have heard from the beginning, that you continue to walk in love [guided by it and following it].

2 JOHN 1:6

Yes, You are my Rock and my Fortress; therefore for Your name's sake lead me and guide me.

PSALM 31:3

And He said to them, Come after Me [as disciples—letting Me be your Guide], follow Me, and I will make you fishers of men!

MATTHEW 4:19

Because of and through the heart of tender mercy and loving-kindness of our God, a Light from on high will dawn upon us and visit [us] to shine upon and give light to those who sit in darkness and in the shadow of death, to direct and guide our feet in a straight line into the way of peace.

LUKE 1:78-79

God is my strong Fortress; He guides the blameless in His way and sets him free. He makes my feet like the hinds' [firm and able]; He sets me secure and confident upon the heights.

2 SAMUEL 22:33-34

For this God is our God forever and ever; He will be our guide [even] until death.

PSALM 48:14

Though I may not know what the future holds, I will listen to the voice of God and follow His direction for my life.

BELIEVE IT:

And the Lord shall guide you continually and satisfy you in drought and in dry places and make strong your bones. And you shall be like a watered garden and like a spring of water whose waters fail not.

ISAIAH 58:11

He leads the humble in what is right, and the humble He teaches His way.

PSALM 25:9

You in Your great mercy forsook them not in the wilderness; the pillar of the cloud departed not from them by day to lead them in the way, nor the pillar of fire by night to light the way they should go.

NEHEMIAH 9:19

He makes me lie down in [fresh, tender] green pastures; He leads me beside the still and restful waters. He refreshes and restores my life (my self); He leads me in the paths of righteousness [uprightness and right standing with Him—not for my earning it, but] for His name's sake.

PSALM 23:2-3

For who has known or understood the mind (the counsels and purposes) of the Lord so as to guide and instruct Him and give Him knowledge? But we have the mind of Christ (the Messiah) and do hold the thoughts (feelings and purposes) of His heart.

1 CORINTHIANS 2:16

From the end of the earth will I cry to You, when my heart is overwhelmed and fainting; lead me to the rock that is higher than I [yes, a rock that is too high for me].

PSALM 61:2

Teach me to do Your will, for You are my God; let Your good Spirit lead me into a level country and into the land of uprightness.

PSALM 143:10

He will feed His flock like a shepherd: He will gather the lambs in His arm, He will carry them in His bosom and will gently lead those that have their young.

ISAIAH 40:11

Lead me, O Lord, in Your righteousness because of my enemies; make Your way level (straight and right) before my face.

PSALM 5:8

. . . Your hand lead me, and Your right hand shall hold me.

PSALM 139:10

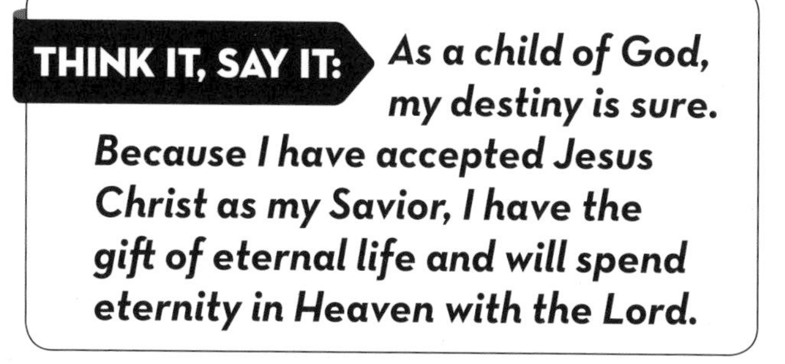

BELIEVE IT:

For God so greatly loved and dearly prized the world that He [even] gave up His only begotten (unique) Son, so that whoever believes in (trusts in, clings to, relies on) Him shall not perish (come to destruction, be lost) but have eternal (everlasting) life.

JOHN 3:16

And He answered him, Truly I tell you, today you shall be with Me in Paradise.

LUKE 23:43

God will wipe away every tear from their eyes; and death shall be no more, neither shall there be anguish (sorrow and mourning) nor grief nor pain any more, for the old conditions and the former order of things have passed away.

REVELATION 21:4

But the truth is that they were yearning for and aspiring to a better and more desirable country, that is, a heavenly [one]. For that reason God is not ashamed to be called their God [even to be surnamed their God—the God of Abraham, Isaac, and Jacob], for He has prepared a city for them.

HEBREWS 11:16

But, on the contrary, as the Scripture says, What eye has not seen and ear has not heard and has not entered into the heart of man, [all that] God has prepared (made and keeps ready) for those who love Him [who hold Him in affectionate reverence, promptly obeying Him and gratefully recognizing the benefits He has bestowed].

1 CORINTHIANS 2:9

I saw no temple in the city, for the Lord God Omnipotent [Himself] and the Lamb [Himself] are its temple. And the city has no need of the sun nor of the moon to give light to it, for the splendor and radiance (glory) of God illuminate it, and the Lamb is its lamp.

REVELATION 21:22-23

But we look for new heavens and a new earth according to His promise, in which righteousness (uprightness, freedom from sin, and right standing with God) is to abide.

2 PETER 3:13

Then they will go away into eternal punishment, but those who are just and upright and in right standing with God into eternal life.

MATTHEW 25:46

The sheep that are My own hear and are listening to My voice; and I know them, and they follow Me. And I give them eternal life, and they shall never lose it or perish throughout the ages. [To all eternity they shall never by any means be destroyed.] And no one is able to snatch them out of My hand.

JOHN 10:27-28

For we know that if the tent which is our earthly home is destroyed (dissolved), we have from God a building, a house not made with hands, eternal in the heavens.

2 CORINTHIANS 5:1

So then, we are always full of good and hopeful and confident courage; we know that while we are at home in the body, we are abroad from the home with the Lord [that is promised us].

2 CORINTHIANS 5:6

And he who overcomes (is victorious) and who obeys My commands to the [very] end [doing the works that please Me], I will give him authority and power over the nations.

REVELATION 2:26

CHAPTER 6

What am I going to Believe about OVERCOMING DIFFICULTIES?

Many Christians lose hope and give up the minute they are faced with opposition. They don't know what the Word of God says about dealing with tough circumstances so they run at the first sign of trouble.

The Bible never promises that we won't have trouble. As a matter of fact, it says just the opposite. Jesus said in John 16:33 that we would have "tribulation and trials and distress." If that was the end of the verse, that would be pretty depressing. But the verse goes on to say that we should "be of good cheer" for He has "overcome the world."

Whatever difficulty you are facing today, remember that Jesus has overcome the world. Stand strong and refuse to give up. Keep pressing forward—thinking, saying and believing with determination and confidence that the Lord will deliver you.

I will not give up just because a situation is difficult. Trials will come in this world, but Jesus is my Deliverer.

BELIEVE IT:

I have told you these things, so that in Me you may have [perfect] peace and confidence. In the world you have tribulation and trials and distress and frustration; but be of good cheer [take courage; be confident, certain, undaunted]! For I have overcome the world. [I have deprived it of power to harm you and have conquered it for you.]

JOHN 16:33

Blessed (happy, to be envied) is the man who is patient under trial and stands up under temptation, for when he has stood the test and been approved, he will receive [the victor's] crown of life which God has promised to those who love Him.

JAMES 1:12

And he who overcomes (is victorious) and who obeys My commands to the [very] end [doing the works that please Me], I will give him authority and power over the nations.

REVELATION 2:26

For no temptation (no trial regarded as enticing to sin), [no matter how it comes or where it leads] has overtaken you and laid hold on you that is not common to man [that is, no temptation or trial has come to you that is beyond human resistance and that is not adjusted and adapted and belonging to human experience, and such as man can bear]. But God is faithful [to His Word and to His compassionate nature], and He [can be trusted] not to let you be tempted and tried and assayed beyond your ability and strength of resistance and power to endure, but with the temptation He will [always] also provide the way out (the means of escape to a landing place), that you may be capable and strong and powerful to bear up under it patiently.

1 CORINTHIANS 10:13

Consider it wholly joyful, my brethren, whenever you are enveloped in or encounter trials of any sort or fall into various temptations. Be assured and understand that the trial and proving of your faith bring out endurance and steadfastness and patience. But let endurance and steadfastness and patience have full play and do a thorough work, so that you may be [people] perfectly and fully developed [with no defects], lacking in nothing.

JAMES 1:2-4

Therefore my brethren, whom I love and yearn to see, my delight and crown (wreath of victory), thus stand firm in the Lord, my beloved.

PHILIPPIANS 4:1

My strength is found in the Lord, not my circumstances.

BELIEVE IT:

There is no [human] wisdom or understanding or counsel [that can prevail] against the Lord. The horse is prepared for the day of battle, but deliverance and victory are of the Lord.

PROVERBS 21:30-31

Through and with God we shall do valiantly, for He it is Who shall tread down our adversaries.

PSALM 108:13

O Lord, give victory; let the King answer us when we call.

PSALM 20:9

The Lord God is my Strength, my personal bravery, and my invincible army; He makes my feet like hinds' feet and will make me to walk [not to stand still in terror, but to walk] and make [spiritual] progress upon my high places [of trouble, suffering, or responsibility]!

HABAKKUK 3:19

Only in the Lord shall one say, I have righteousness (salvation and victory) and strength [to achieve]. To Him shall all come who were incensed against Him, and they shall be ashamed.

ISAIAH 45:24

But He said to me, My grace (My favor and loving-kindness and mercy) is enough for you [sufficient against any danger and enables you to bear the trouble manfully]; for My strength and power are made perfect (fulfilled and completed) and show themselves most effective in [your] weakness. Therefore, I will all the more gladly glory in my weaknesses and infirmities, that the strength and power of Christ (the Messiah) may rest (yes, may pitch a tent over and dwell) upon me! So for the sake of Christ, I am well pleased and take pleasure in infirmities, insults, hardships, persecutions, perplexities and distresses; for when I am weak [in human strength], then am I [truly] strong (able, powerful in divine strength).

2 CORINTHIANS 12:9-10

Fear not [there is nothing to fear], for I am with you; do not look around you in terror and be dismayed, for I am your God. I will strengthen and harden you to difficulties, yes, I will help you; yes, I will hold you up and retain you with My [victorious] right hand of rightness and justice.

ISAIAH 41:10

Whatever I face today, I will not face it alone. I know God is with me, and He has promised to fight my battles for me.

BELIEVE IT:

Contend, O Lord, with those who contend with me; fight against those who fight against me! Take hold of shield and buckler, and stand up for my help! Draw out also the spear and javelin and close up the way of those who pursue and persecute me. Say to me, I am your deliverance!

PSALM 35:1-3

He will swallow up death [in victory; He will abolish death forever]. And the Lord God will wipe away tears from all faces; and the reproach of His people He will take away from off all the earth; for the Lord has spoken it.

ISAIAH 25:8

And the Lord shall save and give victory to the tents of Judah first, that the glory of the house of David and the glory of the inhabitants of Jerusalem may not be magnified and exalted above Judah.

ZECHARIAH 12:7

Jesus said to her, I am [Myself] the Resurrection and the Life. Whoever believes in (adheres to, trusts in, and relies on) Me, although he may die, yet he shall live.

JOHN 11:25

A bruised reed He will not break, and a smoldering (dimly burning) wick He will not quench, till He brings justice and a just cause to victory.

MATTHEW 12:20

When you go forth to battle against your enemies and see horses and chariots and an army greater than your own, do not be afraid of them, for the Lord your God, Who brought you out of the land of Egypt, is with you. And when you come near to the battle, the priest shall approach and speak to the men, And shall say to them, Hear, O Israel, you draw near this day to battle against your enemies. Let not your [minds and] hearts faint; fear not, and do not tremble or be terrified [and in dread] because of them. For the Lord your God is He Who goes with you to fight for you against your enemies to save you. And the officers shall speak to the people, saying, What man is there who has built a new house and has not dedicated it? Let him return to his house, lest he die in the battle and another man dedicate it.

DEUTERONOMY 20:1-5

. . . and the Lord saved by a great victory and deliverance.

1 CHRONICLES 11:14

It is not God's will for me to be defeated and in despair. I am an overcomer because in Christ, I am more than a conqueror!

BELIEVE IT:

Who is it that is victorious over [that conquers] the world but he who believes that Jesus is the Son of God [who adheres to, trusts in, and relies on that fact]?

1 JOHN 5:5

Little children, you are of God [you belong to Him] and have [already] defeated and overcome them [the agents of the antichrist], because He Who lives in you is greater (mightier) than he who is in the world.

1 JOHN 4:4

I have been crucified with Christ [in Him I have shared His crucifixion]; it is no longer I who live, but Christ (the Messiah) lives in me; and the life I now live in the body I live by faith in (by adherence to and reliance on and complete trust in) the Son of God, Who loved me and gave Himself up for me.

GALATIANS 2:20

And they have overcome (conquered) him by means of the blood of the Lamb and by the utterance of their testimony, for they did not love and cling to life even when faced with death [holding their lives cheap till they had to die for their witnessing].

REVELATION 12:11

Yet amid all these things we are more than conquerors and gain a surpassing victory through Him Who loved us.

ROMANS 8:37

So be subject to God. Resist the devil [stand firm against him], and he will flee from you.

JAMES 4:7

And now shall my head be lifted up above my enemies round about me; in His tent I will offer sacrifices and shouting of joy; I will sing, yes, I will sing praises to the Lord.

PSALM 27:6

And You have made them a kingdom (royal race) and priests to our God, and they shall reign [as kings] over the earth!

REVELATION 5:10

In [this] freedom Christ has made us free [and completely liberated us]; stand fast then, and do not be hampered and held ensnared and submit again to a yoke of slavery [which you have once put off].

GALATIANS 5:1

Who gave (yielded) Himself up [to atone] for our sins [and to save and sanctify us], in order to rescue and deliver us from this present wicked age and world order, in accordance with the will and purpose and plan of our God and Father.

GALATIANS 1:4

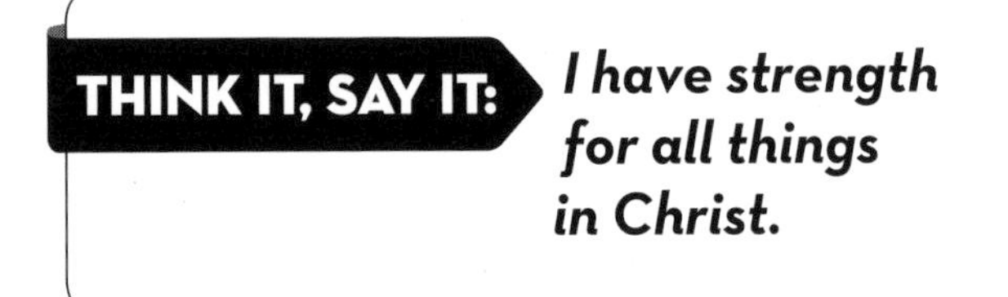

BELIEVE IT:

But the Comforter (Counselor, Helper, Intercessor, Advocate, Strengthener, Standby), the Holy Spirit, Whom the Father will send in My name [in My place, to represent Me and act on My behalf], He will teach you all things. And He will cause you to recall (will remind you of, bring to your remembrance) everything I have told you.

JOHN 14:26

I have strength for all things in Christ Who empowers me [I am ready for anything and equal to anything through Him Who infuses inner strength into me; I am self-sufficient in Christ's sufficiency].

PHILIPPIANS 4:13

And whatever you do [no matter what it is] in word or deed, do everything in the name of the Lord Jesus and in [dependence upon] His Person, giving praise to God the Father through Him.

COLOSSIANS 3:17

In conclusion, be strong in the Lord [be empowered through your union with Him]; draw your strength from Him [that strength which His boundless might provides].

EPHESIANS 6:10

Therefore put on God's complete armor, that you may be able to resist and stand your ground on the evil day [of danger], and, having done all [the crisis demands], to stand [firmly in your place].

EPHESIANS 6:13

Then I heard a strong (loud) voice in heaven, saying, Now it has come—the salvation and the power and the kingdom (the dominion, the reign) of our God, and the power (the sovereignty, the authority) of His Christ (the Messiah); for the accuser of our brethren, he who keeps bringing before our God charges against them day and night, has been cast out!

REVELATION 12:10

For You have been a shelter and a refuge for me, a strong tower against the adversary.

PSALM 61:3

THINK IT, SAY IT: ***I will get up and press on no matter how many times it seems like I'm knocked down.***

BELIEVE IT:

For a righteous man falls seven times and rises again, but the wicked are overthrown by calamity.

PROVERBS 24:16

Yet I will rejoice in the Lord; I will exult in the [victorious] God of my salvation!

HABAKKUK 3:18

Therefore then, since we are surrounded by so great a cloud of witnesses [who have borne testimony to the Truth], let us strip off and throw aside every encumbrance (unnecessary weight) and that sin which so readily (deftly and cleverly) clings to and entangles us, and let us run with patient endurance and steady and active persistence the appointed course of the race that is set before us.

HEBREWS 12:1

Is anyone among you afflicted (ill-treated, suffering evil)? He should pray. Is anyone glad at heart? He should sing praise [to God].

JAMES 5:13

For the weapons of our warfare are not physical [weapons of flesh and blood], but they are mighty before God for the overthrow and destruction of strongholds.

2 CORINTHIANS 10:4

But thanks be to God, Who gives us the victory [making us conquerors] through our Lord Jesus Christ. Therefore, my beloved brethren, be firm (steadfast), immovable, always abounding in the work of the Lord [always being superior, excelling, doing more than enough in the service of the Lord], knowing and being continually aware that your labor in the Lord is not futile [it is never wasted or to no purpose].

1 CORINTHIANS 15:57-58

We will [shout in] triumph at your salvation and victory, and in the name of our God we will set up our banners. May the Lord fulfill all your petitions.

PSALM 20:5

For the Lord takes pleasure in His people; He will beautify the humble with salvation and adorn the wretched with victory.

PSALM 149:4

So let us seize and hold fast and retain without wavering the hope we cherish and confess and our acknowledgement of it, for He Who promised is reliable (sure) and faithful to His word.

HEBREWS 10:23

Worrying or being anxious will not solve my problem. I will be at peace, resting and believing God will make a way for me.

BELIEVE IT:

Therefore I tell you, stop being perpetually uneasy (anxious and worried) about your life, what you shall eat or what you shall drink; or about your body, what you shall put on. Is not life greater [in quality] than food, and the body [far above and more excellent] than clothing?

MATTHEW 6:25

But seek (aim at and strive after) first of all His kingdom and His righteousness (His way of doing and being right), and then all these things taken together will be given you besides. So do not worry or be anxious about tomorrow, for tomorrow will have worries and anxieties of its own. Sufficient for each day is its own trouble.

MATTHEW 6:33-34

Anxiety in a man's heart weighs it down, but an encouraging word makes it glad.

PROVERBS 12:25

Behold, I am doing a new thing! Now it springs forth; do you not perceive and know it and will you not give heed to it? I will even make a way in the wilderness and rivers in the desert.

ISAIAH 43:19

Casting the whole of your care [all your anxieties, all your worries, all your concerns, once and for all] on Him, for He cares for you affectionately and cares about you watchfully.

1 PETER 5:7

And who of you by worrying and being anxious can add one unit of measure (cubit) to his stature or to the span of his life?

MATTHEW 6:27

Do not fret or have any anxiety about anything, but in every circumstance and in everything, by prayer and petition (definite requests), with thanksgiving, continue to make your wants known to God.

PHILIPPIANS 4:6

And He came and preached the glad tidings of peace to you who were afar off and [peace] to those who were near.

EPHESIANS 2:17

The Lord will fight for you, and you shall hold your peace and remain at rest.

EXODUS 14:14

I give every obstacle, uncertainty and difficulty over to God. He is in control of my life. I have nothing to fear.

BELIEVE IT:

[Most] blessed is the man who believes in, trusts in, and relies on the Lord, and whose hope and confidence the Lord is. For he shall be like a tree planted by the waters that spreads out its roots by the river; and it shall not see and fear when heat comes; but its leaf shall be green. It shall not be anxious and full of care in the year of drought, nor shall it cease yielding fruit.

JEREMIAH 17:7-8

Be still and rest in the Lord; wait for Him and patiently lean yourself upon Him; fret not yourself because of him who prospers in his way, because of the man who brings wicked devices to pass. Cease from anger and forsake wrath; fret not yourself—it tends only to evildoing.

PSALM 37:7–8

In the multitude of my [anxious] thoughts within me, Your comforts cheer and delight my soul!

PSALM 94:19

But when they deliver you up, do not be anxious about how or what you are to speak; for what you are to say will be given you in that very hour and moment.

MATTHEW 10:19

My desire is to have you free from all anxiety and distressing care . . . .

1 CORINTHIANS 7:32

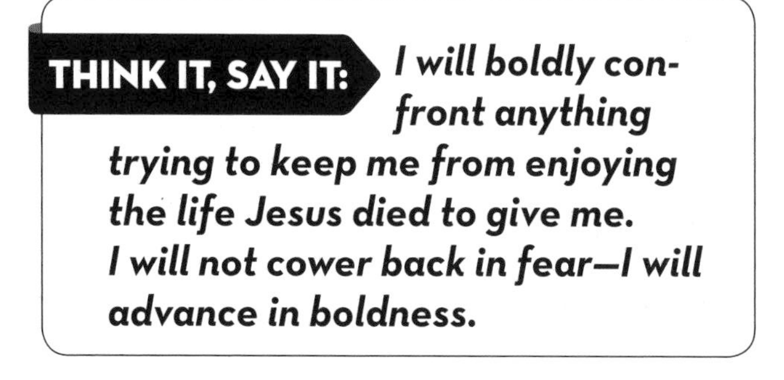

THINK IT, SAY IT: ***I will boldly confront anything trying to keep me from enjoying the life Jesus died to give me. I will not cower back in fear—I will advance in boldness.***

BELIEVE IT:

This is in keeping with my own eager desire and persistent expectation and hope, that I shall not disgrace myself nor be put to shame in anything; but that with the utmost freedom of speech and unfailing courage, now as always heretofore, Christ (the Messiah) will be magnified and get glory and praise in this body of mine and be boldly exalted in my person, whether through (by) life or through (by) death.

PHILIPPIANS 1:20

In the day when I called, You answered me; and You strengthened me with strength (might and inflexibility to temptation) in my inner self.

PSALM 138:3

Let us then fearlessly and confidently and boldly draw near to the throne of grace (the throne of God's unmerited favor to us sinners), that we may receive mercy [for our failures] and find grace to help in good time for every need [appropriate help and well-timed help, coming just when we need it].

HEBREWS 4:16

For I never shrank or kept back or fell short from declaring to you the whole purpose and plan and counsel of God.

ACTS 20:27

But you shall receive power (ability, efficiency, and might) when the Holy Spirit has come upon you, and you shall be My witnesses in Jerusalem and all Judea and Samaria and to the ends (the very bounds) of the earth.

ACTS 1:8

And [pray] also for me, that [freedom of] utterance may be given me, that I may open my mouth to proclaim boldly the mystery of the good news (the Gospel).

EPHESIANS 6:19

As I seek the Lord, He will give me the wisdom I need to make the right choice when faced with a tough decision.

BELIEVE IT:

But it is from Him that you have your life in Christ Jesus, Whom God made our Wisdom from God, [revealed to us a knowledge of the divine plan of salvation previously hidden, manifesting itself as] our Righteousness [thus making us upright and putting us in right standing with God], and our Consecration [making us pure and holy], and our Redemption [providing our ransom from eternal penalty for sin].

1 CORINTHIANS 1:30

Happy (blessed, fortunate, enviable) is the man who finds skillful and godly Wisdom, and the man who gets understanding [drawing it forth from God's Word and life's experiences], For the gaining of it is better than the gaining of silver, and the profit of it better than fine gold.

PROVERBS 3:13-14

But [only] with [God] are [perfect] wisdom and might; He [alone] has [true] counsel and understanding.

JOB 12:13

And the teachers and those who are wise shall shine like the brightness of the firmament, and those who turn many to righteousness (to uprightness and right standing with God) [shall give forth light] like the stars forever and ever.

DANIEL 12:3

If any of you is deficient in wisdom, let him ask of the giving God [Who gives] to everyone liberally and ungrudgingly, without reproaching or faultfinding, and it will be given him.

JAMES 1:5

Look carefully then how you walk! Live purposefully and worthily and accurately, not as the unwise and witless, but as wise (sensible, intelligent people), making the very most of the time [buying up each opportunity], because the days are evil.

EPHESIANS 5:15-16

But the wisdom from above is first of all pure (undefiled); then it is peace-loving, courteous (considerate, gentle). [It is willing to] yield to reason, full of compassion and good fruits; it is wholehearted and straightforward, impartial and unfeigned (free from doubts, wavering, and insincerity).

JAMES 3:17

It is as sport to a [self-confident] fool to do wickedness, but to have skillful and godly Wisdom is pleasure and relaxation to a man of understanding.

PROVERBS 10:23

Let the word [spoken by] Christ (the Messiah) have its home [in your hearts and minds] and dwell in you in [all its] richness, as you teach and admonish and train one another in all insight and intelligence and wisdom [in spiritual things, and as you sing] psalms and hymns and spiritual songs, making melody to God with [His] grace in your hearts.

COLOSSIANS 3:16

A wise man suspects danger and cautiously avoids evil, but the fool bears himself insolently and is [presumptuously] confident.

PROVERBS 14:16

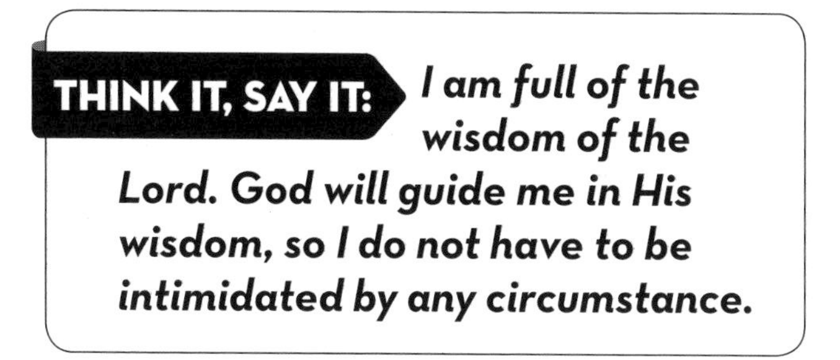

BELIEVE IT:

Oh, the depth of the riches and wisdom and knowledge of God! How unfathomable (inscrutable, unsearchable) are His judgments (His decisions)! And how untraceable (mysterious, undiscoverable) are His ways (His methods, His paths)!

ROMANS 11:33

Skillful and godly Wisdom is more precious than rubies; and nothing you can wish for is to be compared to her.

PROVERBS 3:15

For I [Myself] will give you a mouth and such utterance and wisdom that all of your foes combined will be unable to stand against or refute.

LUKE 21:15

Through skillful and godly Wisdom is a house (a life, a home, a family) built, and by understanding it is established [on a sound and good foundation], and by knowledge shall its chambers [of every area] be filled with all precious and pleasant riches. A wise man is strong and is better than a strong man, and a man of knowledge increases and strengthens his power.

PROVERBS 24:3-5

Forsake not [Wisdom], and she will keep, defend, and protect you; love her, and she will guard you. The beginning of Wisdom is: get Wisdom (skillful and godly Wisdom)! [For skillful and godly Wisdom is the principal thing.] And with all you have gotten, get understanding (discernment, comprehension, and interpretation).

PROVERBS 4:6-7

Apply your mind to instruction and correction and your ears to words of knowledge.

PROVERBS 23:12

And you will know the Truth, and the Truth will set you free.

JOHN 8:32

Call to Me and I will answer you and show you great and mighty things, fenced in and hidden, which you do not know (do not distinguish and recognize, have knowledge of and understand).

JEREMIAH 33:3

The words of a wise man's mouth are gracious and win him favor, but the lips of a fool consume him.

ECCLESIASTES 10:12

How much better it is to get skillful and godly Wisdom than gold! And to get understanding is to be chosen rather than silver.

PROVERBS 16:16

You, through Your commandments, make me wiser than my enemies, for [Your words] are ever before me. I have better understanding and deeper insight than all my teachers, because Your testimonies are my meditation.

PSALM 119:98-99

I have counsel and sound knowledge, I have understanding, I have might and power.

PROVERBS 8:14

When faced with a difficult situation, I will pray, seek wise, godly counsel, and obey the direction God speaks to my heart.

BELIEVE IT:

The way of a fool is right in his own eyes, but he who listens to counsel is wise.

PROVERBS 12:15

The mind of the prudent is ever getting knowledge, and the ear of the wise is ever seeking (inquiring for and craving) knowledge.

PROVERBS 18:15

Hear counsel, receive instruction, and accept correction, that you may be wise in the time to come.

PROVERBS 19:20

Think over these things I am saying [understand them and grasp their application], for the Lord will grant you full insight and understanding in everything.

2 TIMOTHY 2:7

For by wise counsel you can wage your war, and in an abundance of counselors there is victory and safety.

PROVERBS 24:6

The lips of the [uncompromisingly] righteous feed and guide many, but fools die for want of understanding and heart.

PROVERBS 10:21

He who walks [as a companion] with wise men is wise, but he who associates with [self-confident] fools is [a fool himself and] shall smart for it.

PROVERBS 13:20

Where there is no counsel, purposes are frustrated, but with many counselors they are accomplished.

PROVERBS 15:22

He has given food and provision to those who reverently and worshipfully fear Him; He will remember His covenant forever and imprint it [on His mind].

PSALM 111:5

CHAPTER 7

What am I going to Believe about MY FINANCES?

One issue many people deal with on a daily basis is the issue of finances. For many people this is a source of frustration and even defeat because they don't know what the Word of God has to say about money, provision and increase.

No financial resource compares to the wisdom found in God's Word. As believers, we don't have to be uncertain or fearful when it comes to the issue of money, because God has given us financial strategies and guidance in the Scriptures.

No matter what the economy may look like, and no matter what your bank account may say, stand on the promises of God, believing with your thoughts, words and actions that what He says about His provision for your life is the truth.

THINK IT, SAY IT: ***The Lord is my provider. I have nothing to fear.***

BELIEVE IT:

But if God so clothes the grass of the field, which today is alive and green and tomorrow is tossed into the furnace, will He not much more surely clothe you? . . .

MATTHEW 6:30

But you shall [earnestly] remember the Lord your God, for it is He Who gives you power to get wealth . . . .

DEUTERONOMY 8:18

The blessing of the Lord—it makes [truly] rich, and He adds no sorrow with it [neither does toiling increase it].

PROVERBS 10:22

. . . I have never seen the godly abandoned or their children begging for bread.

PSALM 37:25 NLT

So Abraham called the name of that place The Lord Will Provide. And it is said to this day, On the mount of the Lord it will be provided.

GENESIS 22:14

Thus says the Lord, your Redeemer, the Holy One of Israel: I am the Lord your God, Who teaches you to profit, Who leads you in the way that you should go.
ISAIAH 48:17

Then you will prosper if you are careful to keep and fulfill the statues and ordinances with which the Lord charged Moses concerning Israel . . . .
1 CHRONICLES 22:13

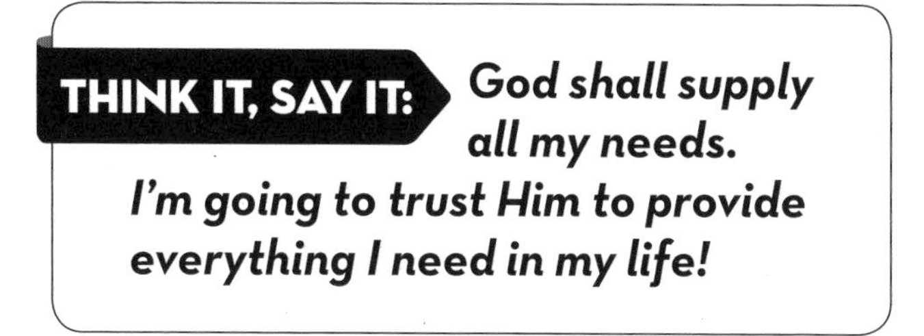

BELIEVE IT:

And you shall eat in plenty and be satisfied and praise the name of the Lord, your God, Who has dealt wondrously with you. And My people shall never be put to shame.
JOEL 2:26

. . . They who seek (inquire of and require) the Lord [by right of their need and on the authority of His Word], none of them shall lack any beneficial thing.
PSALM 34:10

"For I know the plans I have for you," declares the Lord, "plans to prosper you and not to harm you, plans to give you hope and a future.

JEREMIAH 29:11 NIV

And my god will liberally supply (fill to the full) your every need according to His riches in glory in Christ Jesus.

PHILIPPIANS 4:19

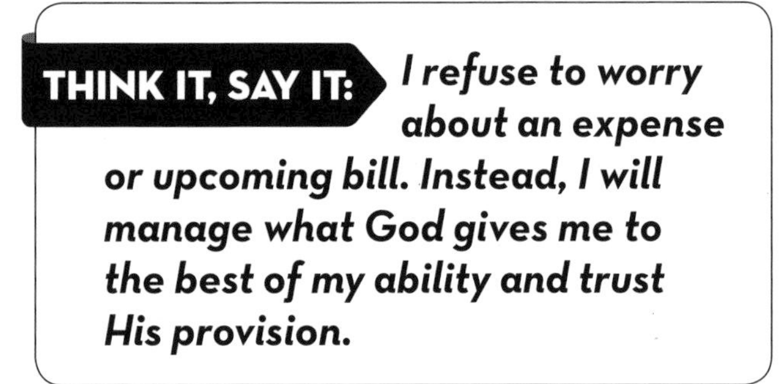

BELIEVE IT:

Do not fret or have any anxiety about anything, but in every circumstance and in everything, by prayer and petition (definite requests), with thanksgiving, continue to make your wants known to God.

PHILIPPIANS 4:6

He has given food and provision to those who reverently and worshipfully fear Him; he will remember His covenant forever and imprint it [on His mind].

PSALM 111:5

Therefore do not worry and be anxious, saying, What are we going to have to eat? or, What are we going to have to wear?

MATTHEW 6:31

And the Lord your God will make you abundantly prosperous in every work of your hand, in the fruit of your body, of your cattle, of your land, for good; for the Lord will again delight in prospering you, as He took delight in your fathers.

DEUTERONOMY 30:9

Abraham said, My son, God Himself will provide . . . .

GENESIS 22:8

So be patient, brethren, [as you wait] till the coming of the Lord. See how the farmer waits expectantly for the precious harvest from the land. [See how] he keeps up his patient [vigil] over it until it receives the early and late rains.

JAMES 5:7

For in Him does our heart rejoice, because we have trusted (relied on and been confident) in His holy name. Let Your mercy and loving-kindness, O Lord, be upon us, in proportion to our waiting and hoping for You.

PSALM 33:21-22

And He led them on safely and in confident trust, so that they feared not . . . .

PSALM 78:53

God is the Source of everything I need and He wants to bless me. I will seek Him, obey His Word, and trust Him to provide whatever I need.

BELIEVE IT:

May the Lord, the God of your fathers, make you a thousand times as many as you are and bless you as He has promised you!

DEUTERONOMY 1:11

The Lord is my Shepherd [to feed, guide, and shield me], I shall not lack.

PSALM 23:1

He who did not withhold or spare [even] His own Son but gave Him up for us all, will He not also with Him freely and graciously give us all [other] things?

ROMANS 8:32

If you . . . know how to give good and advantageous gifts to your children, how much more will your Father Who is in heaven [perfect as He is] give good and advantageous things to those who keep on asking Him!

MATTHEW 7:11

And God is able to make all grace (every favor and earthly blessing) come to you in abundance, so that you may always and under all circumstances and whatever the need be self-sufficient [possessing enough to require no aid or support and furnished in abundance for every good work and charitable donation].

2 CORINTHIANS 9:8

And [God] Who provides seed for the sower and bread for eating will also provide and multiply your [resources for] sowing and increase the fruits of your righteousness [which manifests itself in active goodness, kindness, and charity].

2 CORINTHIANS 9:10

. . . I came that they may have and enjoy life, and have it in abundance (to the full, till it overflows).

JOHN 10:10

And therefore the Lord [earnestly] waits [expecting, looking, and longing] to be gracious to you; and therefore He lifts Himself up, that He may have mercy on you and show loving-kindness to you. For the Lord is a God of justice. Blessed (happy, fortunate, to be envied) are all those who [earnestly] wait for Him, who expect and look and long for Him [for His victory, His favor, His love, His peace, His joy, and His matchless, unbroken companionship]!

ISAIAH 30:18

As God blesses me, I choose to be a blessing to others every chance I get.

BELIEVE IT:

May the Lord give you increase more and more, you and your children. May you be blessed of the Lord, Who made heaven and earth!

PSALM 115:14-15

. . . The same Lord is Lord over all [of us] and He generously bestows His riches upon all who call upon Him [in faith].

ROMANS 10:12

Now to Him Who, by (in consequence of) the [action of His] power that is at work within us, is able to [carry out His purpose and] do superabundantly, far over and above all that we [dare] ask or think [infinitely beyond our highest prayers, desires, thoughts, hopes, or dreams].

EPHESIANS 3:20

Yes, the Lord will give what is good, and our land will yield its increase.

PSALM 85:12

For out of His fullness (abundance) we have all received [all had a share and we were all supplied with] one grace after another and spiritual blessing upon spiritual blessing and even favor upon favor and gift [heaped] upon gift.
JOHN 1:16

Enlarge the place of your tent, and let the curtains of your habitations be stretched out; spare not; lengthen your cords and strengthen your stakes.
ISAIAH 54:2

THINK IT, SAY IT: ***I will pray for God's favor in my life and remember His promises to bless me and provide what I need.***

BELIEVE IT:

For no matter how many promises God has made, they are "Yes" in Christ. And so through him the "Amen" is spoken by us to the glory of God.
2 CORINTHIANS 1:20 NIV

In the morning, Lord, you hear my voice; in the morning I lay my requests before you and wait expectantly.
PSALM 5:3 NIV

Bless (affectionately, gratefully praise) the Lord, O my soul, and forget not [one of] all His benefits.

PSALM 103:2

And whatever you ask for in prayer, having faith and [really] believing, you will receive.

MATTHEW 21:22

No good thing will He withhold from those who walk uprightly.

PSALM 84:11

Fully satisfied and assured that God was able and mighty to keep His word and to do what He had promised.

ROMANS 4:21

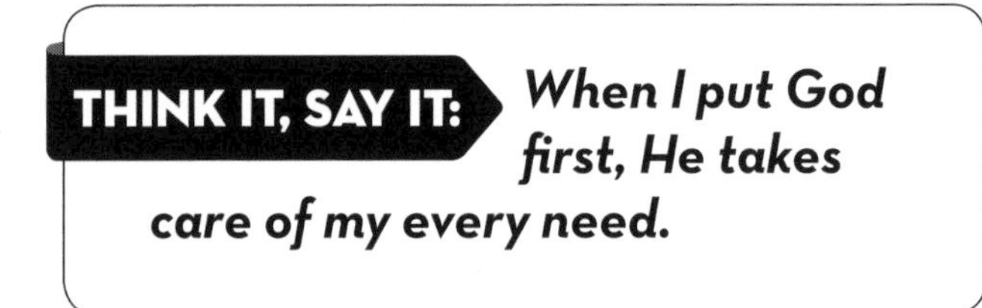

BELIEVE IT:

. . . Gather and heap up and store for yourselves treasures in heaven, where neither moth nor rust nor worm consume and destroy, and where thieves do not break through and steal; for where your treasure is, there will your heart be also.

MATTHEW 6:20-21

This Book of the Law shall not depart out of your mouth, but you shall meditate on it day and night, that you may observe and do according to all that is written in it. For then you shall make your way prosperous, and then you shall deal wisely and have good success.

JOSHUA 1:8

But seek (aim at and strive after) first of all His kingdom and His righteousness (His way of doing and being right), and then all these things taken together will be given you besides.

MATTHEW 6:33

He set himself to seek God in the days of Zechariah, who instructed him in the things of God; and as long as he sought (inquired of, yearned for) the Lord, God made him prosper.

2 CHRONICLES 26:5

Come close to God and He will come close to you . . . .

JAMES 4:8

And set your minds and keep them set on what is above (the higher things), not on the things that are on the earth.

COLOSSIANS 3:2

For the eyes of the Lord run to and fro throughout the whole earth to show Himself strong in behalf of those whose hearts are blameless toward Him . . . .

2 CHRONICLES 16:9

If you live in Me [abide vitally united to Me] and My words remain in you and continue to live in your hearts, ask whatever you will, and it shall be done for you.

JOHN 15:7

Then you will seek Me, inquire for, and require Me [as a vital necessity] and find Me when you search for Me with all your heart. I will be found by you, says the Lord . . . .

JEREMIAH 29:13-14

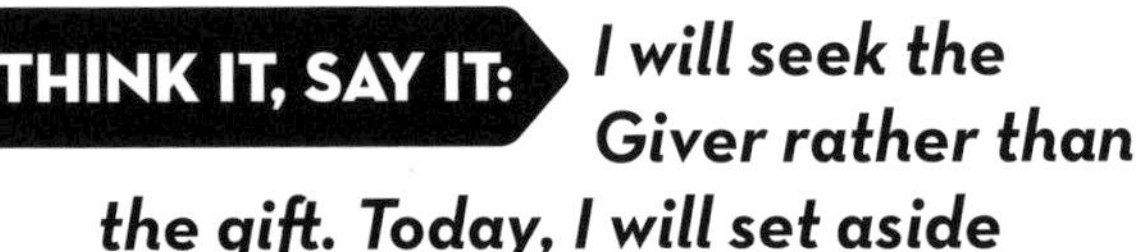

THINK IT, SAY IT: ***I will seek the Giver rather than the gift. Today, I will set aside some time to seek God and thank Him for His goodness in my life.***

BELIEVE IT:

Enter into His gates with thanksgiving and a thank offering and into His courts with praise! Be thankful and say so to Him, bless and affectionately praise His name!

PSALM 100:4

Delight yourself also in the Lord, and He will give you the desires and secret petitions of your heart.

PSALM 37:4

If you will listen diligently to the voice of the Lord your God, being watchful to do all His commandments . . . all these blessings shall come upon you and overtake you if you heed the voice of the Lord your God.
DEUTERONOMY 28:1-2

You have said, Seek My face [inquire for and require My presence as your vital need]. My heart says to You, Your face (Your presence), Lord, will I seek, inquire for, and require [of necessity and on the authority of Your Word].
PSALM 27:8

But as for you . . . aim and pursue righteousness (right standing with God and true goodness), godliness (which is the loving fear of God and being Christlike), faith, love, steadfastness (patience), and gentleness of heart.
1 TIMOTHY 6:11

I am looking and waiting for the Lord more than watchmen for the morning, I say, more than watchmen for the morning.
PSALM 130:6

I waited patiently and expectantly for the Lord; and He inclined to me and heard my cry.
PSALM 40:1

I can reach out and be a blessing to others because God is taking care of my needs.

BELIEVE IT:

. . . God loves (He takes pleasure in, prizes above other things, and is unwilling to abandon or to do without) a cheerful (joyous, "prompt to do it") giver [whose heart is in his giving].

2 CORINTHIANS 9:7

But when you give to charity, do not let your left hand know what your right hand is doing, so that your deeds of charity may be in secret; and your Father Who sees in secret will reward you openly.

MATTHEW 6:3-4

Contribute to the needs of God's people [sharing in the necessities of the saints]; pursue the practice of hospitality.

ROMANS 12:13

For God is not unrighteous to forget or overlook your labor and the love which you have shown for His name's sake in ministering to the needs of the saints . . . .

HEBREWS 6:10

In everything I have pointed out to you [by example] that, by working diligently in this manner, we ought to assist the weak, being mindful of the words of the Lord Jesus, how He Himself said, It is more blessed (makes one happier and more to be envied) to give than to receive.

ACTS 20:35

Whoever is kind to the poor lends to the Lord, and he will reward them for what they have done.

PROVERBS 19:17 NIV

I am an ambassador of Christ Jesus. Today I will bless others and demonstrate God's love.

BELIEVE IT:

We are therefore Christ's ambassadors, as though God were making his appeal through us . . . .

2 CORINTHIANS 5:20 NIV

Do not forget or neglect to do kindness and good, to be generous and distribute and contribute to the needy [of the church as embodiment and proof of fellowship], for such sacrifices are pleasing to God.

HEBREWS 13:16

A generous person will prosper; whoever refreshes others will be refreshed.

PROVERBS 11:25 NIV

And if you pour out that with which you sustain your own life for the hungry and satisfy the need of the afflicted, then shall your light rise in darkness . . . And the Lord shall guide you continually and satisfy you in drought and in dry places and make strong your bones. And you shall be like a watered garden and like a spring of water whose waters fail not.

ISAIAH 58:10-11

. . . Truly I tell you in so far as you did it for one of the least [in the estimation of men] of these My brethren, you did it for Me.

MATTHEW 25:40

But thanks be to God, Who in Christ always leads us in triumph [as trophies of Christ's victory] and through us spreads and makes evident the fragrance of the knowledge of God everywhere, for we are the sweet fragrance of Christ [which exhales] unto God, [discernible alike] among those who are being saved and among those who are perishing.

2 CORINTHIANS 2:14-15

Beloved, if God loved us so [very much], we also ought to love one another.

1 JOHN 4:11

I am going to find a way to help someone in my life today. I am going to give an encouraging word, lend a helping hand or meet a need.

BELIEVE IT:

Give, and it will be given to you. A good measure, pressed down, shaken together and running over, will be poured into your lap. For with the measure you use, it will be measured to you.

LUKE 6:38 NIV

Contribute to the needs of God's people [sharing in the necessities of the saints]; pursue the practice of hospitality.

ROMANS 12:13

. . . Jesus went around doing good and healing all who were oppressed by the devil, for God was with him.

ACTS 10:38 NLT

For we are God's [own] handiwork (His workmanship), recreated in Christ Jesus, [born anew] that we may do those good works . . . .

EPHESIANS 2:10

Blessed are those who are generous, because they feed the poor.

PROVERBS 22:9 NLT

Not so shall it be among you; but whoever wishes to be great among you must be your servant.

MATTHEW 20:26

THINK IT, SAY IT: ***The pursuit of money is not the answer to all my problems. God's love for me is the answer I'm looking for.***

BELIEVE IT:

Listen, my beloved brethren: Has not God chosen those who are poor in the eyes of the world to be rich in faith and in their position as believers and to inherit the kingdom which He has promised to those who love Him?

JAMES 2:5

But those who crave to be rich fall into temptation and a snare and into many foolish (useless, godless) and hurtful desires that plunge men into ruin and destruction and miserable perishing.

1 TIMOTHY 6:9

He who leans on, trusts in, and is confident in his riches shall fall, but the [uncompromisingly] righteous shall flourish like a green bough.

PROVERBS 11:28

No servant is able to serve two masters; for either he will hate the one and love the other, or he will stand by and be devoted to the one and despise the other. You cannot serve God and mammon (riches, or anything in which you trust and on which you rely).

LUKE 16:13

Riches provide no security in any day of wrath and judgment, but righteousness (uprightness and right standing with God) delivers from death.

PROVERBS 11:4

For what does it profit a man to gain the whole world, and forfeit his life [in the eternal kingdom of God]?

MARK 8:36

For the Father Himself [tenderly] loves you because you have loved Me and have believed that I came out from the Father.

JOHN 16:27

I give you a new commandment: that you should love one another. Just as I have loved you, so you too should love one another.

JOHN 13:34

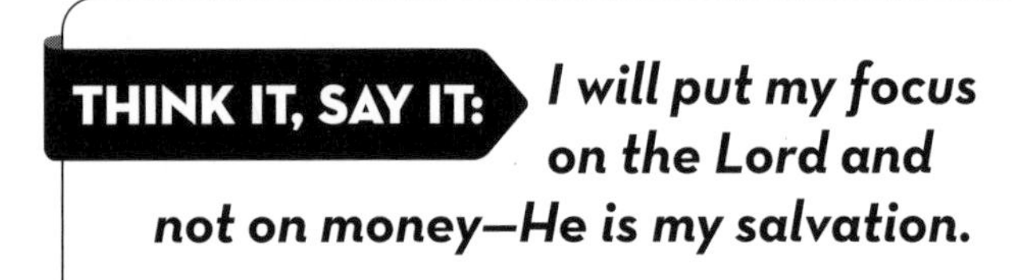

BELIEVE IT:

Remove far from me falsehood and lies; give me neither poverty nor riches; feed me with the food that is needful for me, lest I be full and deny You and say, Who is the Lord? Or lest I be poor and steal, and so profane the name of my God.

PROVERBS 30:8-9

As for the rich in this world, charge them not to be proud and arrogant and contemptuous of others, nor to set their hopes on uncertain riches, but on God, Who richly and ceaselessly provides us with everything for [our] enjoyment. [Charge them] to do good, to be rich in good works, to be liberal and generous of heart, ready to share [with others], in this way laying up for themselves [the riches that endure forever as] a good foundation for the future, so that they may grasp that which is life indeed.

1 TIMOTHY 6:17-19

A good name is rather to be chosen than great riches, and loving favor rather than silver and gold.

PROVERBS 22:1

Better is the poor man who walks in his integrity than he who willfully goes in double and wrong ways, though he is rich.

PROVERBS 28:6

The rich man is wise in his own eyes and conceit, but the poor man who has understanding will find him out.

PROVERBS 28:11

And when Jesus heard it, He said to him, One thing you still lack. Sell everything that you have and divide [the money] among the poor, and you will have [rich] treasure in heaven; and come back [and] follow Me [become My disciple, join My party, and accompany Me]. But when he heard this, he became distressed and very sorrowful, for he was rich—exceedingly so.

LUKE 18:22-23

The rich and poor meet together; the Lord is the Maker of them all.

PROVERBS 22:2

[And it is, indeed, a source of immense profit, for] godliness accompanied with contentment (that contentment which is a sense of inward sufficiency) is great and abundant gain. For we brought nothing into the world, and obviously we cannot take anything out of the world.

1 TIMOTHY 6:6-7

Today, I refuse to worry about money. My trust is in the Lord, and I choose to go through the day believing He will provide any and everything that I need.

BELIEVE IT:

And the Lord shall make you have a surplus of prosperity, through the fruit of your body, of your livestock, and of your ground, in the land which the Lord swore to your fathers to give you.

DEUTERONOMY 28:11

Bring all the tithes (the whole tenth of your income) into the storehouse, that there may be food in My house, and prove Me now by it, says the Lord of hosts, if I will not open the windows of heaven for you and pour you out a blessing, that there shall not be room enough to receive it.

MALACHI 3:10

The Lord shall open to you His good treasury, the heavens, to give the rain of your land in its season and to bless all the work of your hands; and you shall lend to many nations, but you shall not borrow.

DEUTERONOMY 28:12

[Remember] this: he who sows sparingly and grudgingly will also reap sparingly and grudgingly, and he who sows generously [that blessings may come to someone] will also reap generously and with blessings.
2 CORINTHIANS 9:6

The Lord is on my side; I will not fear. What can man do to me? The Lord is on my side and takes my part, He is among those who help me; therefore shall I see my desire established upon those who hate me. It is better to trust and take refuge in the Lord than to put confidence in man.
PSALM 118:6-8

Behold, God, my salvation! I will trust and not be afraid, for the Lord God is my strength and song; yes, He has become my salvation.
ISAIAH 12:2

Indeed, we felt within ourselves that we had received the [very] sentence of death, but that was to keep us from trusting in and depending on ourselves instead of on God Who raises the dead. [For it is He] Who rescued and saved us from such a perilous death, and He will still rescue and save us; in and on Him we have set our hope (our joyful and confident expectation) that He will again deliver us [from danger and destruction and draw us to Himself].
2 CORINTHIANS 1:9-10

Thus says the Lord: Let not the wise and skillful person glory and boast in his wisdom and skill; let not the mighty and powerful person glory and boast in his strength and power; let not the person who is rich [in physical gratification and earthly wealth] glory and boast in his [temporal satisfactions and earthly] riches; but let him who glories glory in this: that he understands and knows Me [personally and practically, directly discerning and recognizing My character], that I am the Lord, Who practices loving-kindness, judgment, and righteousness in the earth, for in these things I delight, says the Lord.

JEREMIAH 9:23-24

He sends forth His word and heals them and rescues them from the pit and destruction.

PSALM 107:20

CHAPTER 8

What am I going to Believe about HEALING?

Many people believe healing is something God did in the Bible but He no longer does today. But believing this way will keep you from experiencing God's healing touch in your life.

The truth is, Jesus can heal us everywhere we hurt. It is His will to see His children walking in complete physical, emotional and spiritual health.

If you need healing, stand on these scriptures and believe what God says about His power to heal. Trust that He is able and willing to completely restore health to every area of your life.

Jesus died so we could enjoy a healthy, whole, and completely restored life in Him.

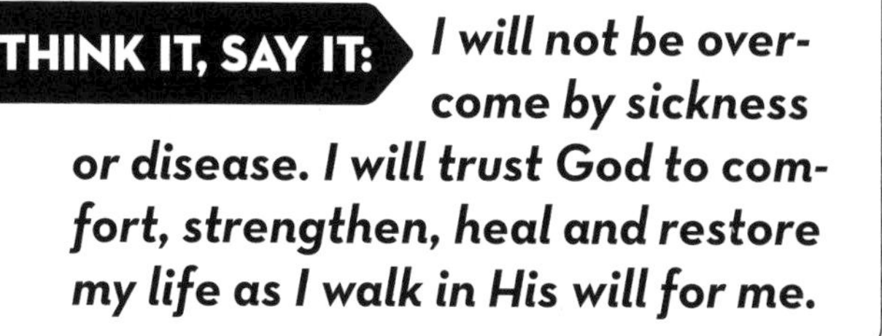
THINK IT, SAY IT: ***I will not be overcome by sickness or disease. I will trust God to comfort, strengthen, heal and restore my life as I walk in His will for me.***

BELIEVE IT:

He sends forth His word and heals them and rescues them from the pit and destruction.

PSALM 107:20

But so much the more the news spread abroad concerning Him, and great crowds kept coming together to hear [Him] and to be healed by Him of their infirmities.

LUKE 5:15

When He went ashore and saw a great throng of people, He had compassion (pity and deep sympathy) for them and cured their sick.

MATTHEW 14:14

And He reached out His hand and touched him, saying, I am willing; be cleansed by being cured. And instantly his leprosy was cured and cleansed.

MATTHEW 8:3

My son, attend to my words; consent and submit to my sayings. Let them not depart from your sight; keep them in the center of your heart. For they are life to those who find them, healing and health to all their flesh.

PROVERBS 4:20-22

You shall serve the Lord your God; He shall bless your bread and water, and I will take sickness from your midst.

EXODUS 23:25

And He went about all Galilee, teaching in their synagogues and preaching the good news (Gospel) of the kingdom, and healing every disease and every weakness and infirmity among the people. So the report of Him spread throughout all Syria, and they brought Him all who were sick, those afflicted with various diseases and torments, those under the power of demons, and epileptics, and paralyzed people, and He healed them.

MATTHEW 4:23-24

The Lord will perfect that which concerns me; Your mercy and loving-kindness, O Lord, endure forever—forsake not the works of Your own hands.

PSALM 138:8

For it is God who works in you to will and to act in order to fulfill his good purpose.

PHILIPPIANS 2:13 NIV

Sickness is not welcome in my body. I am healed by the stripes of Jesus and receive that healing today.

BELIEVE IT:

But He was wounded for our transgressions, He was bruised for our guilt and iniquities; the chastisement [needful to obtain] peace and well-being for us was upon Him, and with the stripes [that wounded] Him we are healed and made whole.

ISAIAH 53:5

He personally bore our sins in His [own] body on the tree [as on an altar and offered Himself on it], that we might die (cease to exist) to sin and live to righteousness. By His wounds you have been healed.

1 PETER 2:24

Bless (affectionately, gratefully praise) the Lord, O my soul; and all that is [deepest] within me, bless His holy name! Bless (affectionately, gratefully praise) the Lord, O my soul, and forget not [one of] all His benefits—Who forgives [every one of] all your iniquities, Who heals [each one of] all your diseases.

PSALM 103:1-3

He heals the brokenhearted and binds up their wounds [curing their pains and their sorrows].
PSALM 147:3

The blind receive their sight and the lame walk, lepers are cleansed (by healing) and the deaf hear, the dead are raised up and the poor have good news (the Gospel) preached to them.
MATTHEW 11:5

When evening came, they brought to Him many who were under the power of demons, and He drove out the spirits with a word and restored to health all who were sick. And thus He fulfilled what was spoken by the prophet Isaiah, He Himself took [in order to carry away] our weaknesses and infirmities and bore away our diseases.
MATTHEW 8:16-17

Nevertheless, I will bring health and healing to it; I will heal my people and will let them enjoy abundant peace and security.
JEREMIAH 33:6 NIV

Who forgives [every one of] all your iniquities, Who heals [each one of] all your diseases.
PSALM 103:3

And the Lord will take away from you all sickness . . . .
DEUTERONOMY 7:15

Today I will walk in complete physical, emotional and spiritual health, glorifying God in my life. The Word of God, not my circumstances defines my future.

BELIEVE IT:

But unto you who revere and worshipfully fear My name shall the Sun of Righteousness arise with healing in His wings and His beams, and you shall go forth and gambol like calves [released] from the stall and leap for joy.

MALACHI 4:2

And all the multitude were seeking to touch Him, for healing power was all the while going forth from Him and curing them all [saving them from severe illnesses or calamities].

LUKE 6:19

So He replied to them, Go and tell John what you have seen and heard: the blind receive their sight, the lame walk, the lepers are cleansed, the deaf hear, the dead are raised up, and the poor have the good news (the Gospel) preached to them.

LUKE 7:22

Be not wise in your own eyes; reverently fear and worship the Lord and turn [entirely] away from evil. It shall be health to your nerves and sinews, and marrow and moistening to your bones.

PROVERBS 3:7-8

Heal me, O Lord, and I shall be healed; save me, and I shall be saved, for You are my praise.

JEREMIAH 17:14

And behold, a woman who had suffered from a flow of blood for twelve years came up behind Him and touched the fringe of His garment; for she kept saying to herself, If I only touch His garment, I shall be restored to health. Jesus turned around and, seeing her, He said, Take courage, daughter! Your faith has made you well. And at once the woman was restored to health.

MATTHEW 9:20-22

How God anointed and consecrated Jesus of Nazareth with the [Holy] Spirit and with strength and ability and power; how He went about doing good and, in particular, curing all who were harassed and oppressed by [the power of] the devil, for God was with Him.

ACTS 10:38

This is my comfort and consolation in my affliction: that Your word has revived me and given me life.

PSALM 119:50

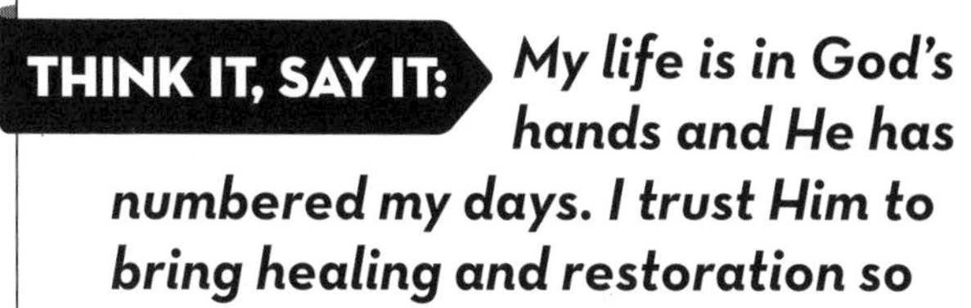

THINK IT, SAY IT: ***My life is in God's hands and He has numbered my days. I trust Him to bring healing and restoration so I can fulfill His plans for me!***

BELIEVE IT:

I shall not die but live, and shall declare the works and recount the illustrious acts of the Lord.

PSALM 118:17

The Lord will strengthen him on his bed of illness; You will sustain him on his sickbed.

PSALM 41:3 NKJV

Beloved, I pray that you may prosper in every way and [that your body] may keep well, even as [I know] your soul keeps well and prospers.

3 JOHN 1:2

And if the Spirit of Him Who raised up Jesus from the dead dwells in you, [then] He Who raised up Christ Jesus from the dead will also restore to life your mortal (short-lived, perishable) bodies through His Spirit Who dwells in you.

ROMANS 8:11

When Jesus received the message, He said, This sickness is not to end in death; but [on the contrary] it is to honor God and to promote His glory, that the Son of God may be glorified through (by) it.

JOHN 11:4

With long life will I satisfy him and show him My salvation.

PSALM 91:16

You have turned my mourning into dancing for me; You have put off my sackcloth and girded me with gladness.

PSALM 30:11

The Lord is close to those who are of a broken heart and saves such as are crushed with sorrow for sin and are humbly and thoroughly penitent.

PSALM 34:18

Yea, though I walk through the [deep, sunless] valley of the shadow of death, I will fear or dread no evil; for You are with me; Your rod [to protect] and Your staff [to guide], they comfort me.

PSALM 23:4

While I live I will praise the LORD; I will sing praises to my God while I have my being.

PSALM 146:2

Jesus has authority over every kind of sickness, weakness and infirmity. He came so I could have life and have it more abundantly!

BELIEVE IT:

And Jesus went about all the cities and villages, teaching in their synagogues and proclaiming the good news (the Gospel) of the kingdom and curing all kinds of disease and every weakness and infirmity.
MATTHEW 9:35

And a great multitude came to Him, bringing with them the lame, the maimed, the blind, the dumb, and many others, and they put them down at His feet; and He cured them.
MATTHEW 15:30

Then shall your light break forth like the morning, and your healing (your restoration and the power of a new life) shall spring forth speedily; your righteousness (your rightness, your justice, and your right relationship with God) shall go before you [conducting you to peace and prosperity], and the glory of the Lord shall be your rear guard.
ISAIAH 58:8

Peace, peace, to him who is far off [both Jew and Gentile] and to him who is near! says the Lord; I create the fruit of his lips, and I will heal him [make his lips blossom anew with speech in thankful praise].
ISAIAH 57:19

And when Jesus went into Peter's house, He saw his mother-in-law lying ill with a fever. He touched her hand and the fever left her; and she got up and began waiting on Him.
MATTHEW 8:14-15

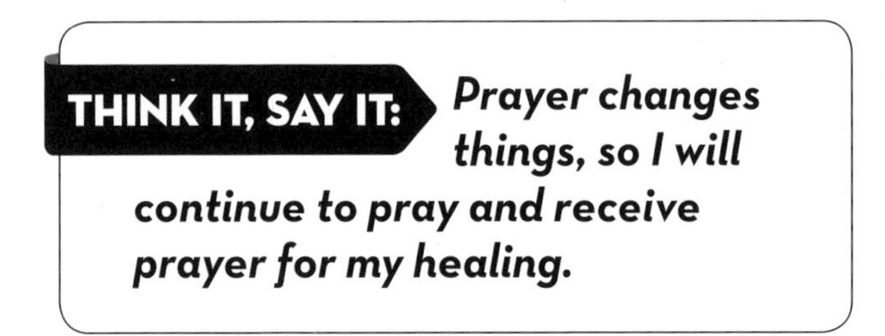

BELIEVE IT:

Therefore humble yourselves [demote, lower yourselves in your own estimation] under the mighty hand of God, that in due time He may exalt you, casting the whole of your care [all your anxieties, all your worries, all your concerns, once and for all] on Him, for He cares for you affectionately and cares about you watchfully.
1 PETER 5:6-7

Is anyone among you sick? He should call in the church elders (the spiritual guides). And they should pray over him, anointing him with oil in the Lord's name. And the prayer [that is] of faith will save him who is sick, and the Lord will restore him; and if he has committed sins, he will be forgiven.

JAMES 5:14-15

If My people, who are called by My name, shall humble themselves, pray, seek, crave, and require of necessity My face and turn from their wicked ways, then will I hear from heaven, forgive their sin, and heal their land.

2 CHRONICLES 7:14

And these attesting signs will accompany those who believe: in My name they will drive out demons; they will speak in new languages; they will pick up serpents; and [even] if they drink anything deadly, it will not hurt them; they will lay their hands on the sick, and they will get well.

MARK 16:17-18

Confess to one another therefore your faults (your slips, your false steps, your offenses, your sins) and pray [also] for one another, that you may be healed and restored [to a spiritual tone of mind and heart]. The earnest (heartfelt, continued) prayer of a righteous man makes tremendous power available [dynamic in its working].

JAMES 5:16

First of all, then, I admonish and urge that petitions, prayers, intercessions, and thanksgivings be offered on behalf of all men.

1 TIMOTHY 2:1

The power of God's Word brings total healing to my life—spiritually, emotionally, mentally, and physically.

BELIEVE IT:

For God did not give us a spirit of timidity (of cowardice, of craven and cringing and fawning fear), but [He has given us a spirit] of power and of love and of calm and well-balanced mind and discipline and self-control.

2 TIMOTHY 1:7

Why are you cast down, O my inner self? And why should you moan over me and be disquieted within me? Hope in God and wait expectantly for Him, for I shall yet praise Him, my Help and my God.

PSALM 42:5

When the righteous cry for help, the Lord hears, and delivers them out of all their distress and troubles.

PSALM 34:17

Come to Me, all you who labor and are heavy-laden and overburdened, and I will cause you to rest. [I will ease and relieve and refresh your souls.]
MATTHEW 11:28

A happy heart is good medicine and a cheerful mind works healing, but a broken spirit dries up the bones.
PROVERBS 17:22

And be constantly renewed in the spirit of your mind [having a fresh mental and spiritual attitude], and put on the new nature (the regenerate self) created in God's image, [Godlike] in true righteousness and holiness.
EPHESIANS 4:23-24

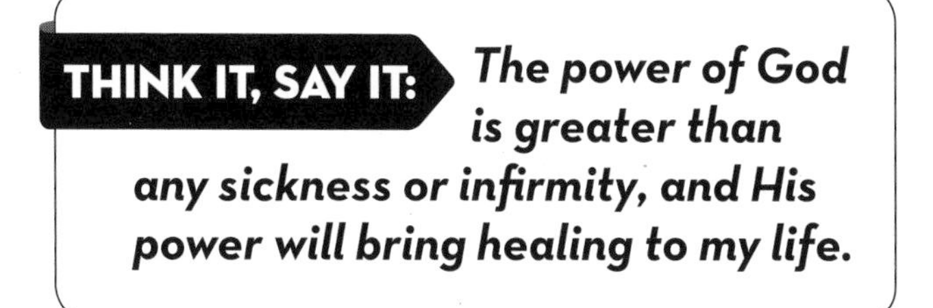

BELIEVE IT:

Yours, O Lord, is the greatness and the power and the glory and the victory and the majesty, for all that is in the heavens and the earth is Yours; Yours is the kingdom, O Lord, and Yours it is to be exalted as Head over all.
1 CHRONICLES 29:11

For with God nothing is ever impossible and no word from God shall be without power or impossible of fulfillment.

LUKE 1:37

But Jesus looked at them and said, With men this is impossible, but all things are possible with God.

MATTHEW 19:26

Fear not [there is nothing to fear], for I am with you; do not look around you in terror and be dismayed, for I am your God. I will strengthen and harden you to difficulties, yes, I will help you; yes, I will hold you up and retain you with My [victorious] right hand of rightness and justice.

ISAIAH 41:10

I know that You can do all things, and that no thought or purpose of Yours can be restrained or thwarted.

JOB 42:2

Alas, Lord God! Behold, You have made the heavens and the earth by Your great power and by Your outstretched arm! There is nothing too hard or too wonderful for You.

JEREMIAH 32:17

Declaring the end and the result from the beginning, and from ancient times the things that are not yet done, saying, My counsel shall stand, and I will do all My pleasure and purpose.

ISAIAH 46:10

Is anything too hard or too wonderful for the Lord? . . .
GENESIS 18:14

He determines and counts the number of the stars;
He calls them all by their names.
PSALM 147:4

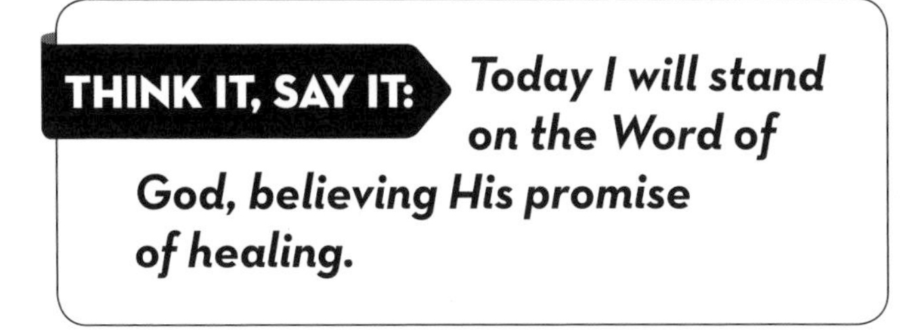

BELIEVE IT:

. . . For truly I say to you, if you have faith [that is living] like a grain of mustard seed, you can say to this mountain, Move from here to yonder place, and it will move; and nothing will be impossible to you.
MATTHEW 17:20

For this reason I am telling you, whatever you ask for in prayer, believe (trust and be confident) that it is granted to you, and you will [get it].
MARK 11:24

Jesus turned around and, seeing her, He said, Take courage, daughter! Your faith has made you well. And at once the woman was restored to health.
MATTHEW 9:22

Jesus said to him, Because you have seen Me, Thomas, do you now believe (trust, have faith)? Blessed and happy and to be envied are those who have never seen Me and yet have believed and adhered to and trusted and relied on Me.

JOHN 20:29

And He said to him, Get up and go on your way. Your faith (your trust and confidence that spring from your belief in God) has restored you to health.

LUKE 17:19

And Jesus said, [You say to Me], If You can do anything? [Why,] all things can be (are possible) to him who believes!

MARK 9:23

The apostles said to the Lord, Increase our faith (that trust and confidence that spring from our belief in God).

LUKE 17:5

When He reached the house and went in, the blind men came to Him, and Jesus said to them, Do you believe that I am able to do this? They said to Him, Yes, Lord. Then He touched their eyes, saying, According to your faith and trust and reliance [on the power invested in Me] be it done to you.

MATTHEW 9:28-29

While I wait for my healing, I will not give up hope. I believe God is going to do something good in my life.

BELIEVE IT:

I wait for the Lord, I expectantly wait, and in His word do I hope.

PSALM 130:5

Have you not known? Have you not heard? The everlasting God, the Lord, the Creator of the ends of the earth, does not faint or grow weary; there is no searching of His understanding. He gives power to the faint and weary, and to him who has no might He increases strength [causing it to multiply and making it to abound].

ISAIAH 40:28-29

Yes, let none who trust and wait hopefully and look for You be put to shame or be disappointed; let them be ashamed who forsake the right or deal treacherously without cause. Show me Your ways, O Lord; teach me Your paths.

PSALM 25:3-4

Our inner selves wait [earnestly] for the Lord; He is our Help and our Shield.

PSALM 33:20

But this I recall and therefore have I hope and expectation: It is because of the Lord's mercy and loving-kindness that we are not consumed, because His [tender] compassions fail not. They are new every morning; great and abundant is Your stability and faithfulness.

LAMENTATIONS 3:21-23

Guide me in Your truth and faithfulness and teach me, for You are the God of my salvation; for You [You only and altogether] do I wait [expectantly] all the day long.

PSALM 25:5

[What, what would have become of me] had I not believed that I would see the Lord's goodness in the land of the living! Wait and hope for and expect the Lord; be brave and of good courage and let your heart be stout and enduring. Yes, wait for and hope for and expect the Lord.

PSALM 27:13-14

The eyes of all wait for You [looking, watching, and expecting] and You give them their food in due season. You open Your hand and satisfy every living thing with favor.

PSALM 145:15-16

The Lord is my portion or share, says my living being (my inner self); therefore will I hope in Him and wait expectantly for Him. The Lord is good to those who wait hopefully and expectantly for Him, to those who seek Him [inquire of and for Him and require Him by right of necessity and on the authority of God's word].

LAMENTATIONS 3:24-25

For I know the thoughts and plans that I have for you, says the Lord, thoughts and plans for welfare and peace and not for evil, to give you hope in your final outcome.

JEREMIAH 29:11

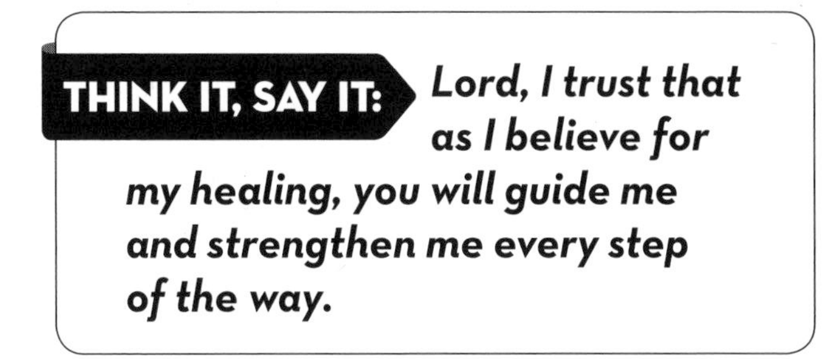

BELIEVE IT:

If any of you is deficient in wisdom, let him ask of the giving God [Who gives] to everyone liberally and ungrudgingly, without reproaching or faultfinding, and it will be given him.

JAMES 1:5

Yes, You are my Rock and my Fortress; therefore for Your name's sake lead me and guide me.
PSALM 31:3

The Lord is my Shepherd [to feed, guide, and shield me], I shall not lack. He makes me lie down in [fresh, tender] green pastures; He leads me beside the still and restful waters. He refreshes and restores my life (my self); He leads me in the paths of righteousness [uprightness and right standing with Him—not for my earning it, but] for His name's sake.
PSALM 23:1-3

And your ears will hear a word behind you, saying, This is the way; walk in it, when you turn to the right hand and when you turn to the left.
ISAIAH 30:21

Your word is a lamp to my feet and a light to my path.
PSALM 119:105

And the Lord shall guide you continually and satisfy you in drought and in dry places and make strong your bones. And you shall be like a watered garden and like a spring of water whose waters fail not.
ISAIAH 58:11

The steps of a [good] man are directed and established by the Lord when He delights in his way [and He busies Himself with his every step].
PSALM 37:23

A man's mind plans his way, but the Lord directs his steps and makes them sure.

PROVERBS 16:9

But when He, the Spirit of Truth (the Truth-giving Spirit) comes, He will guide you into all the Truth (the whole, full Truth). For He will not speak His own message [on His own authority]; but He will tell whatever He hears [from the Father; He will give the message that has been given to Him], and He will announce and declare to you the things that are to come [that will happen in the future].

JOHN 16:13

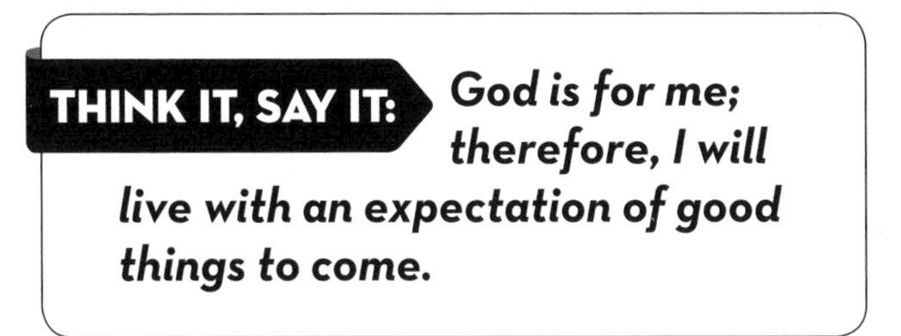

BELIEVE IT:

My soul, wait only upon God and silently submit to Him; for my hope and expectation are from Him. He only is my Rock and my Salvation; He is my Defense and my Fortress, I shall not be moved. With God rests my salvation and my glory; He is my Rock of unyielding strength and impenetrable hardness, and my refuge is in God!

PSALM 62:5-7

Keep and guard me as the pupil of Your eye; hide me in the shadow of Your wings.

PSALM 17:8

According to my earnest expectation and hope that in nothing I shall be ashamed, but with all boldness, as always, so now also Christ will be magnified in my body, whether by life or by death.

PHILIPPIANS 1:20 NKJV

[The Lord] raises the poor out of the dust and lifts the needy from the ash heap and the dung hill, that He may seat them with princes, even with the princes of His people. He makes the barren woman to be a homemaker and a joyful mother of [spiritual] children. Praise the Lord! (Hallelujah!)

PSALM 113:7-9

For in the day of trouble He will hide me in His shelter; in the secret place of His tent will He hide me; He will set me high upon a rock.

PSALM 27:5

When you pass through the waters, I will be with you, and through the rivers, they will not overwhelm you. When you walk through the fire, you will not be burned or scorched, nor will the flame kindle upon you.

ISAIAH 43:2